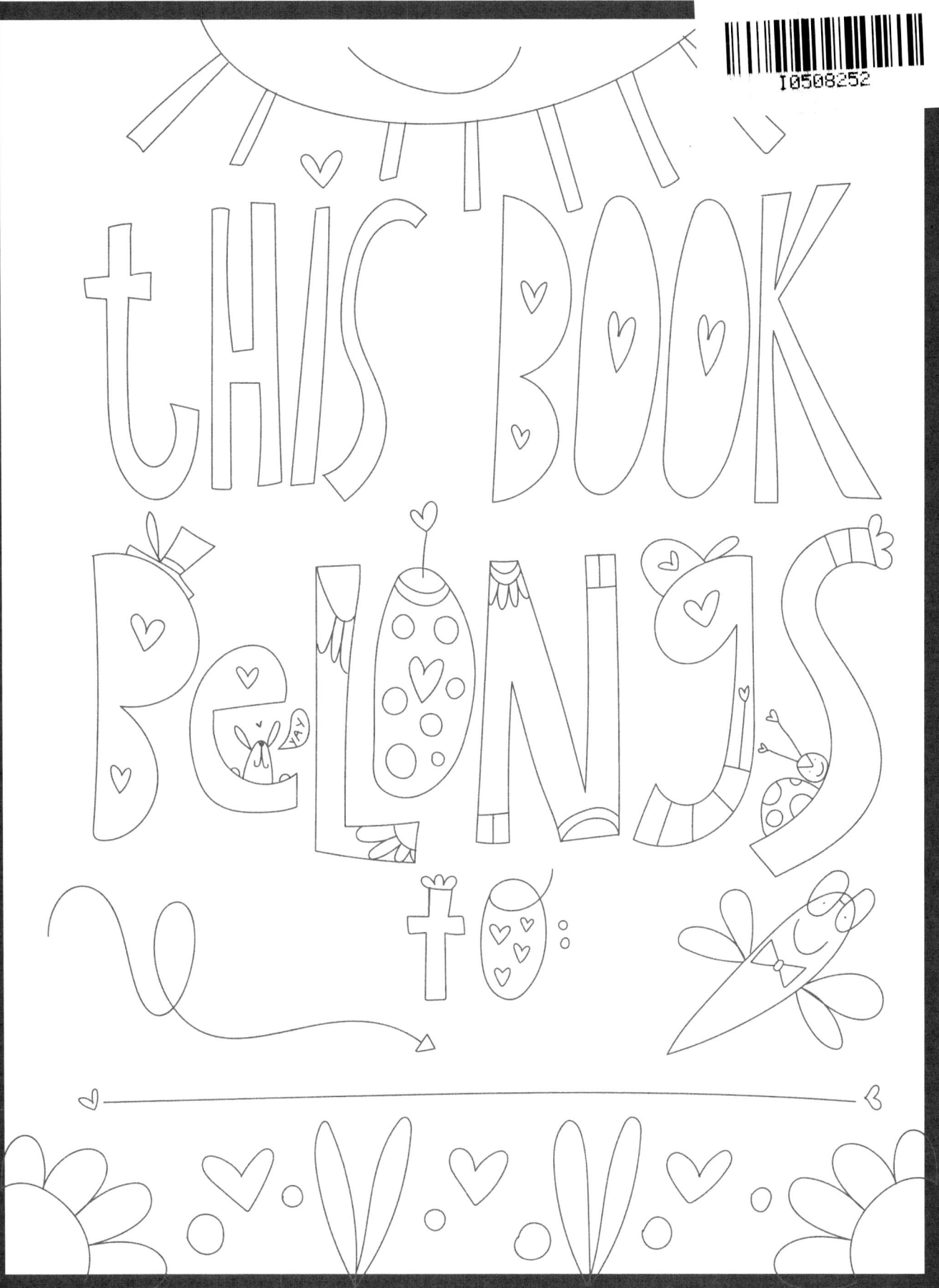

This book is a collection of hand-drawn original illustrations and a great tool to tap into your elevated feelings in a fun, joyful and whimsical way.

To make the most of your coloring session, I invite you to repeat the affirmation while you are coloring, either mentally or out loud - whatever works for you :-).

By repeating the affirmation you will find a way to unwind, relax and feel the peace and joy I have found through art.
It is also a way to think more deeply on the positive message.

Affirmations are a very simple and yet, powerful tool to achieve your best self.
This tool, along with coloring, will bring your subconscious to a new level through an activity that is relaxing, uplifting, and enjoyable.

You may want to cut out the page from the book and put it in a visible place as a reminder to make this whole experience even more effective, inspiring and long-lasting.

I hope you find this book really inspiring. If you want to go deeper please visit my page **isazapata.com/seeds** for small seeds of inspiration.

From my heart to yours!

Isa Zapata
isazapata.com

THANK YOU FOR CHOOSING ISA ZAPATA®

ISA ZAPATA® IS REGISTERED IN THE USA PATENT & TRADEMARK OFFICE

COPYRIGHT © 2021 ISA ZAPATA INC. ALL RIGHTS RESERVED

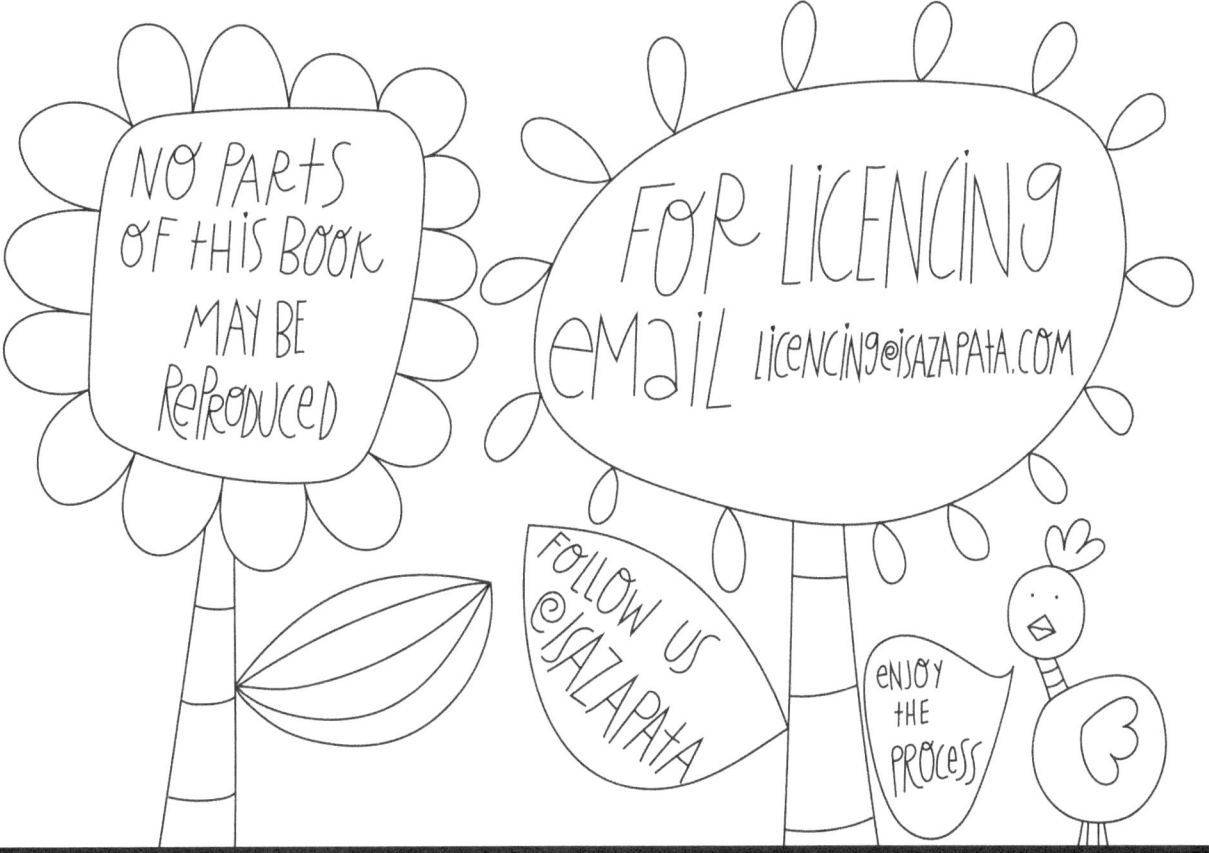

NO PARTS OF THIS BOOK MAY BE REPRODUCED

FOR LICENCING EMAIL licencing@isazapata.com

FOLLOW US @ISAZAPATA

ENJOY THE PROCESS

BE GRATEFUL FOR WHAT
YOU ALREADY HAVE
AND MORE WILL COME

— ISA ZAPATA —

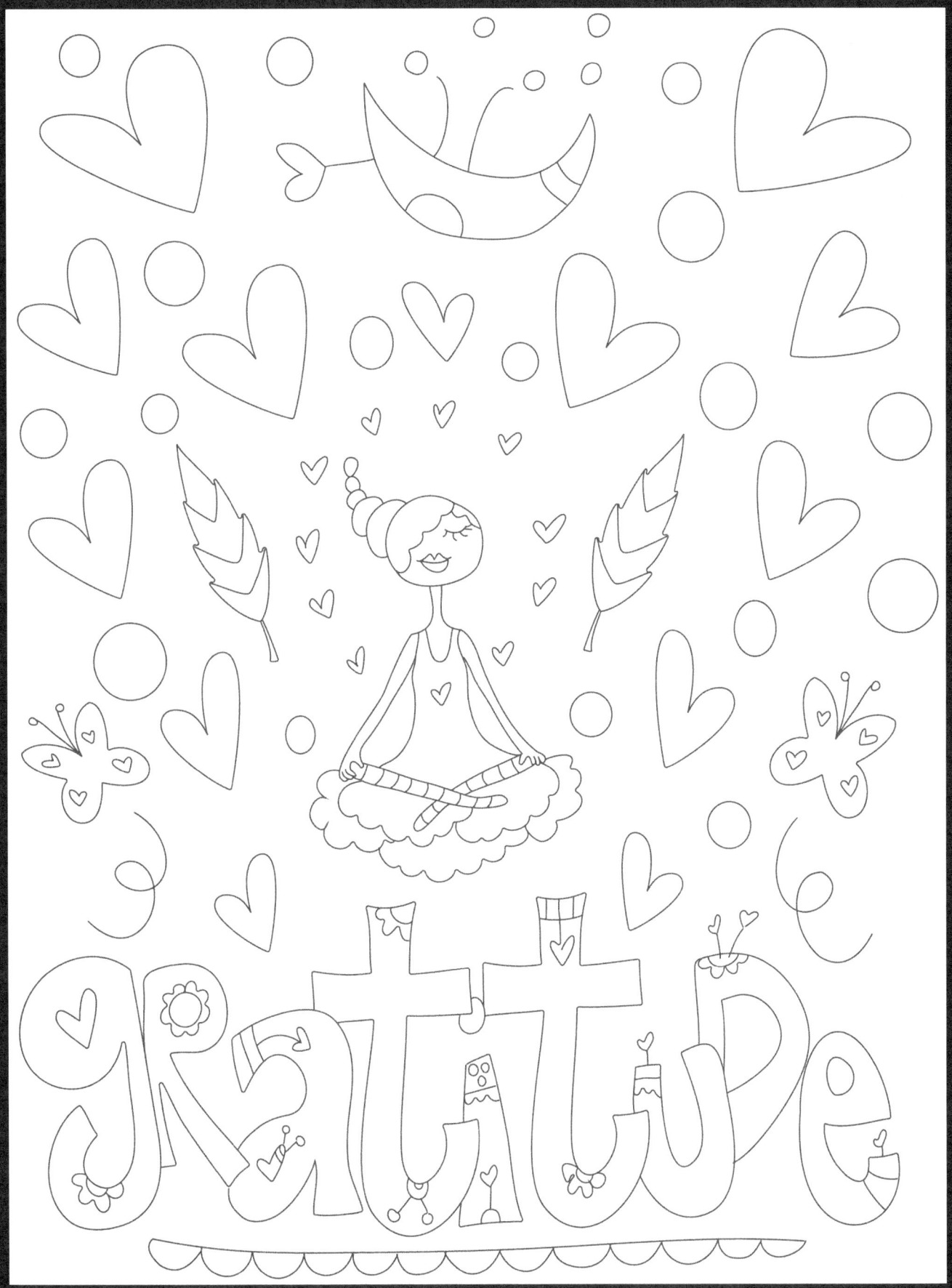

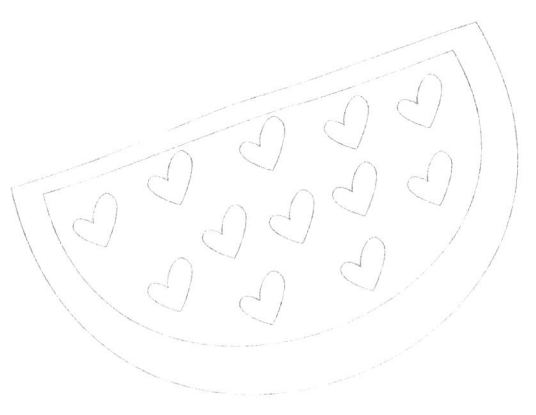

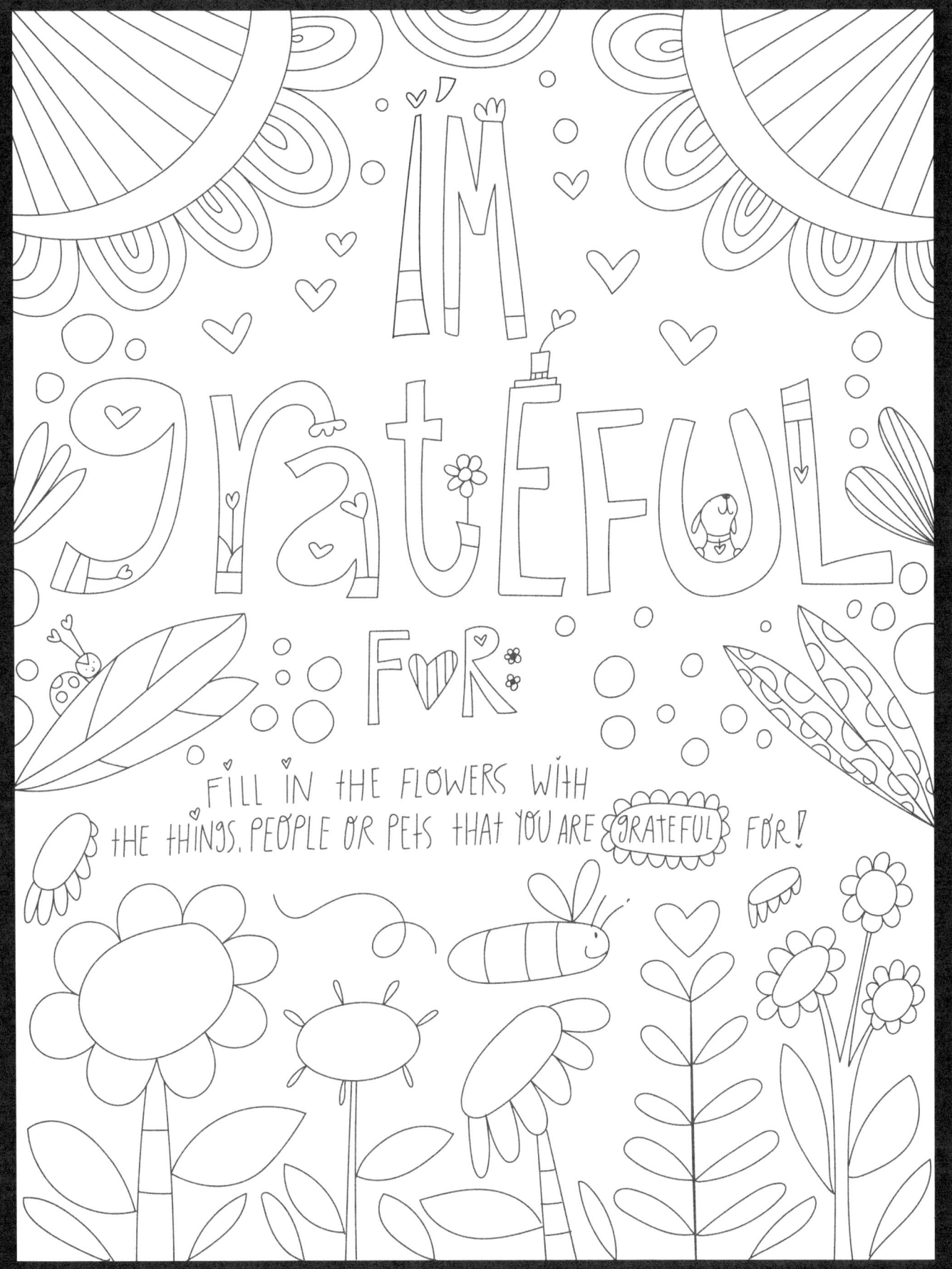

Recognizing and admitting our mistakes takes true courage

— ka zapata —

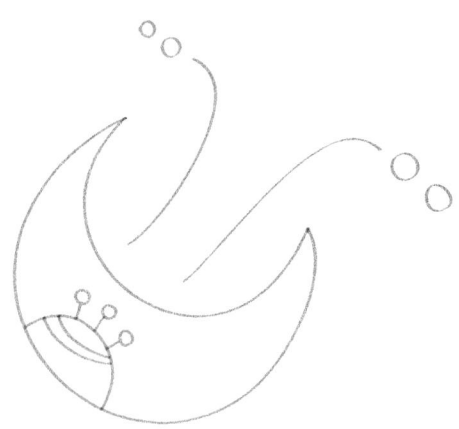

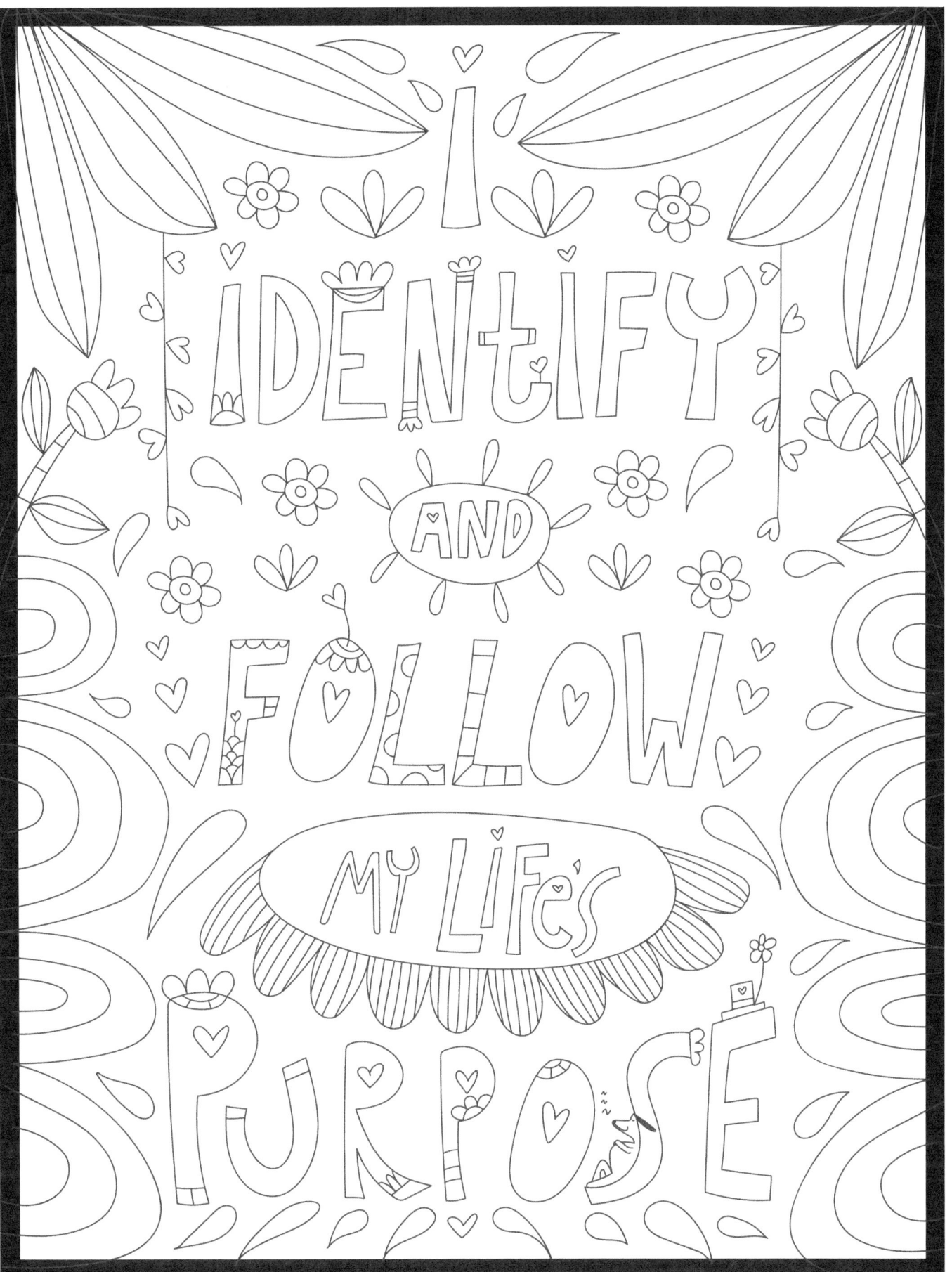

Happiness is created by appreciating the small things in life

— Isa Zapata —

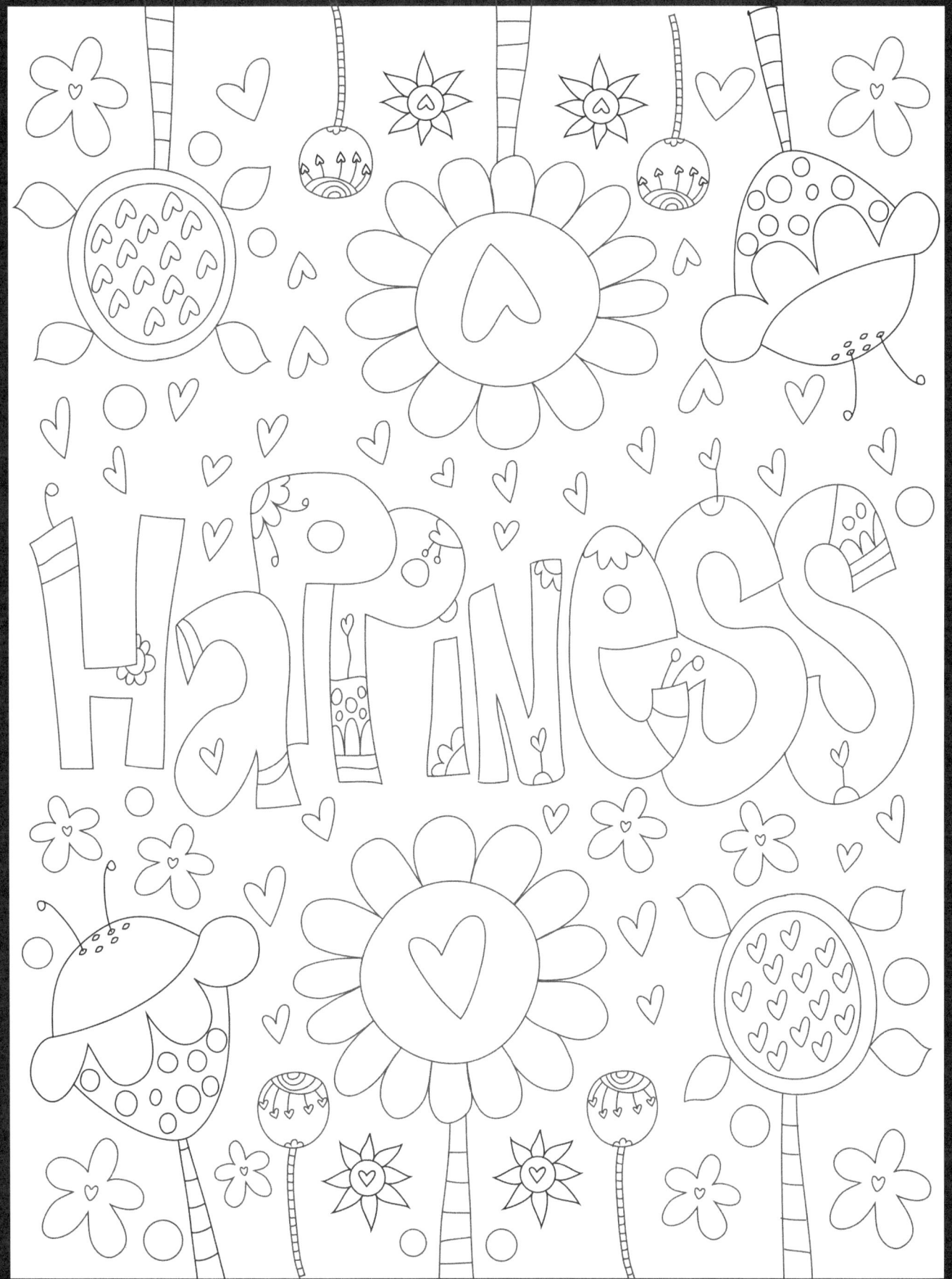

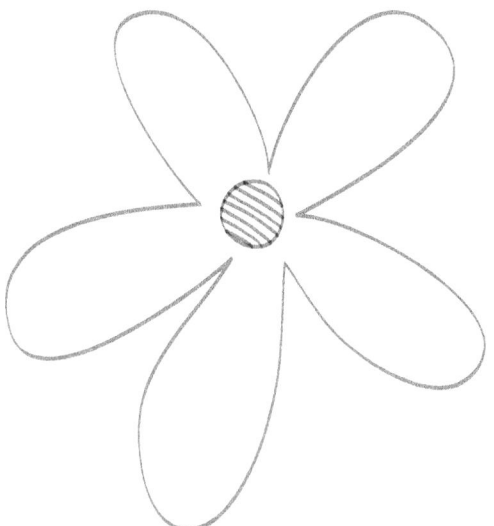

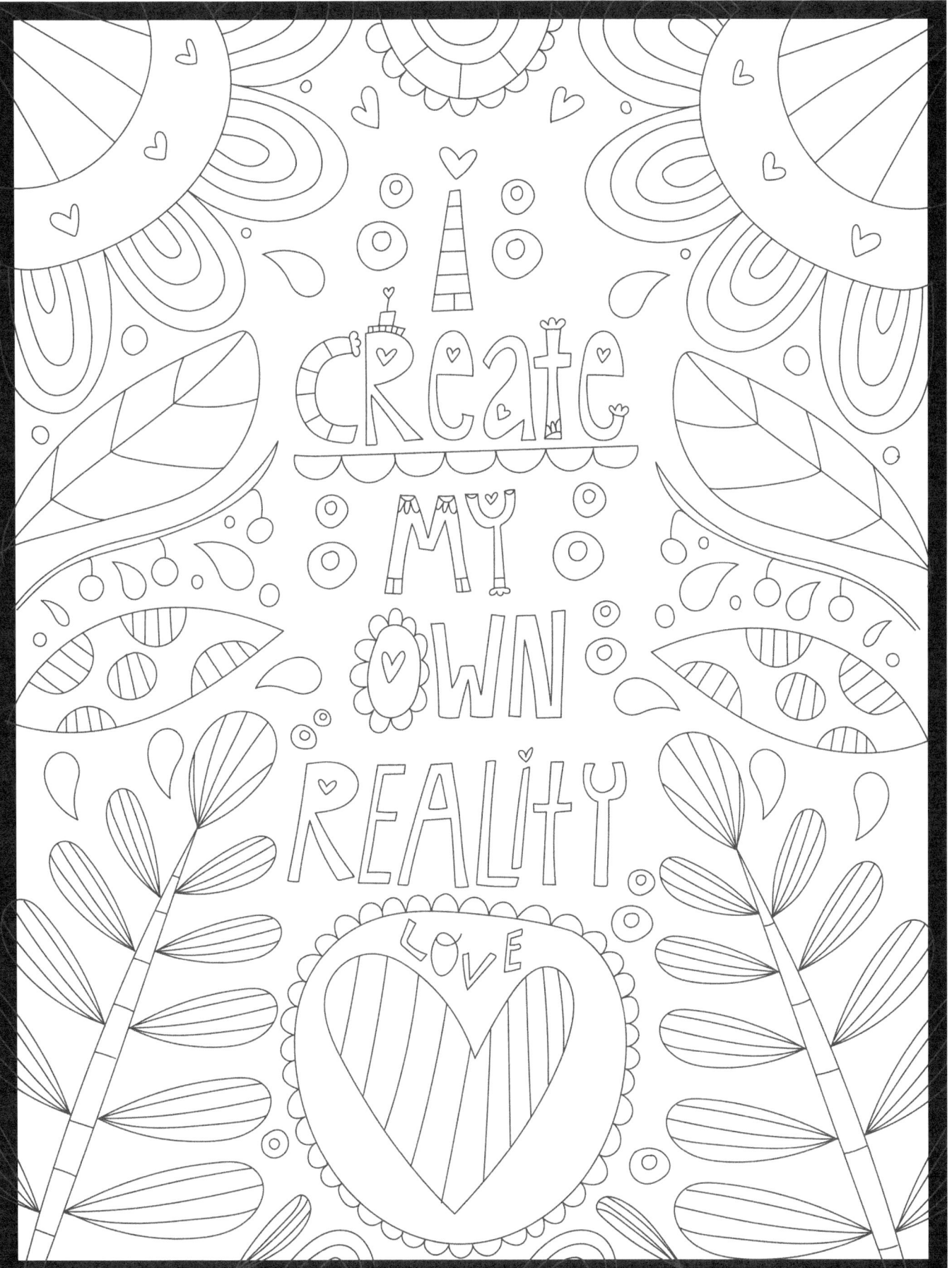

♡

Each day is a new opportunity
to create a better version of yourself.
Make one little change at a time

— Isa Zapata —

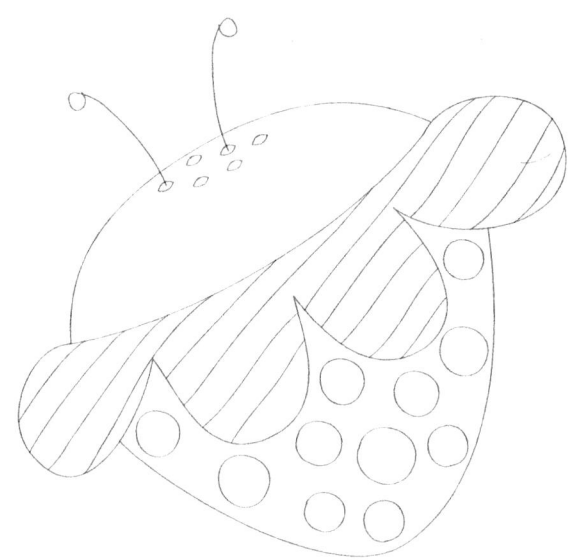

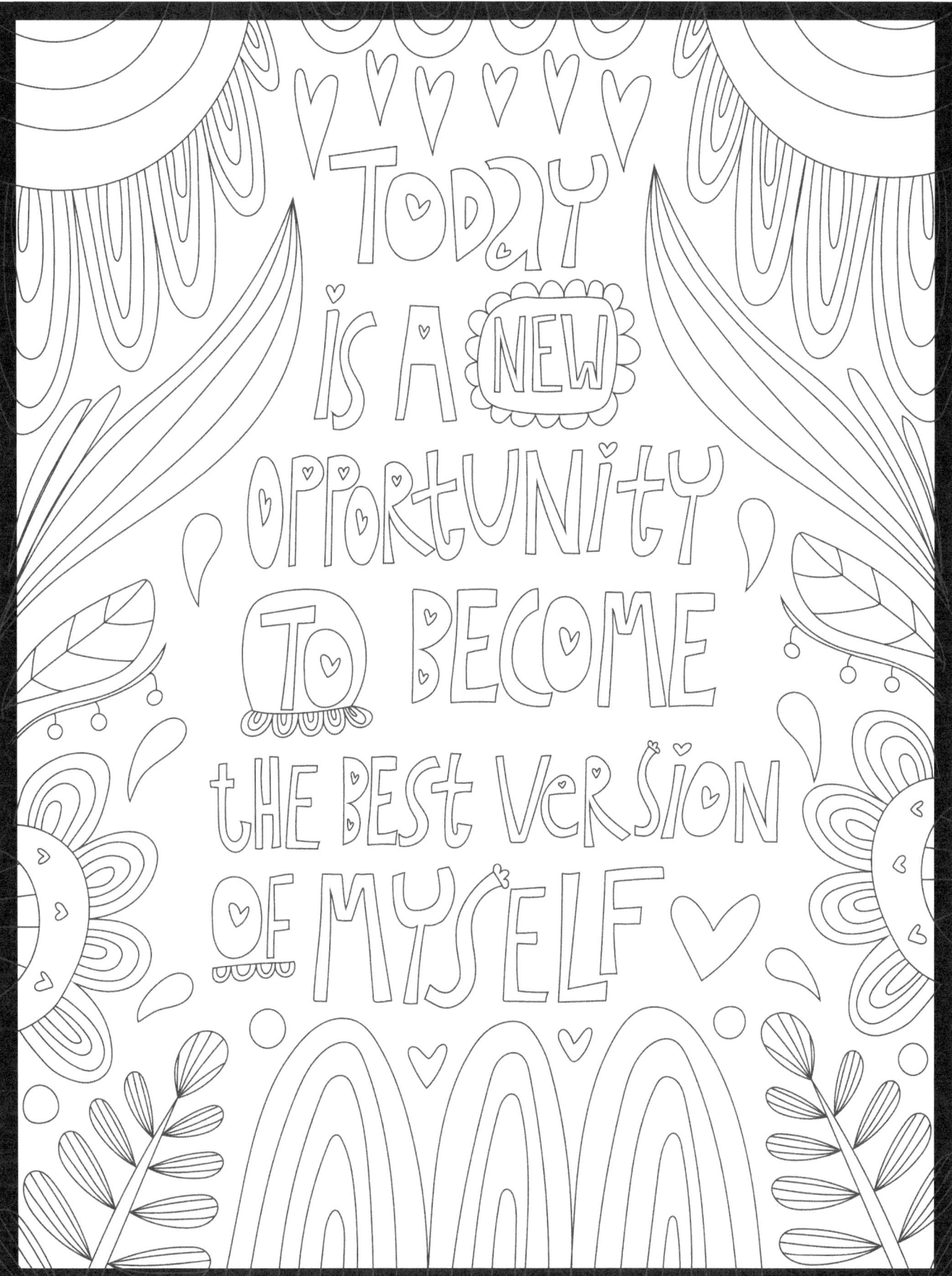

Express your gratitude
with feelings, thoughts and actions

— Isa Zapata —

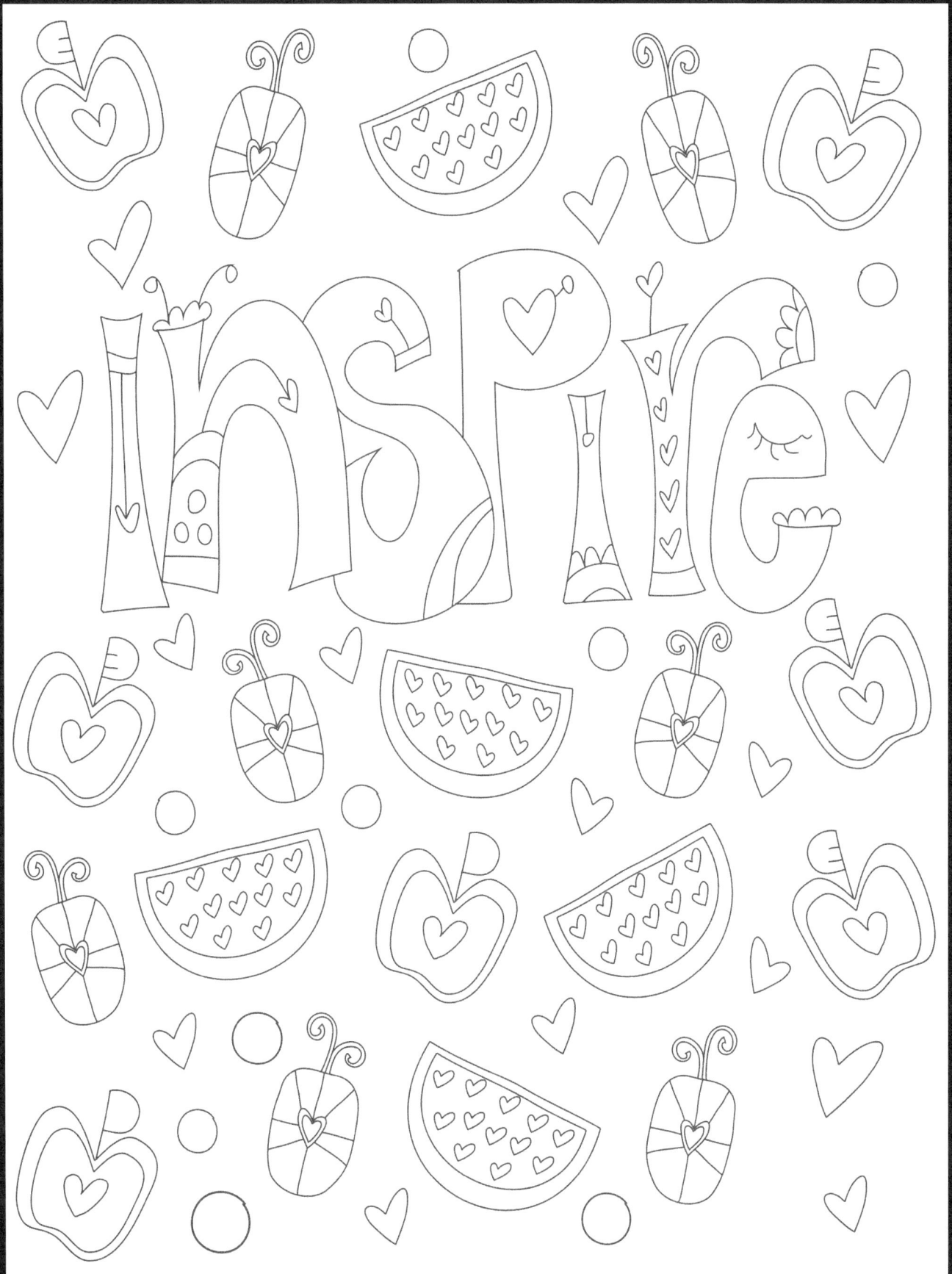

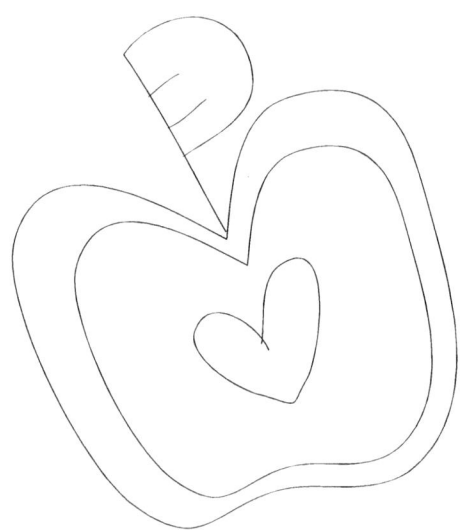

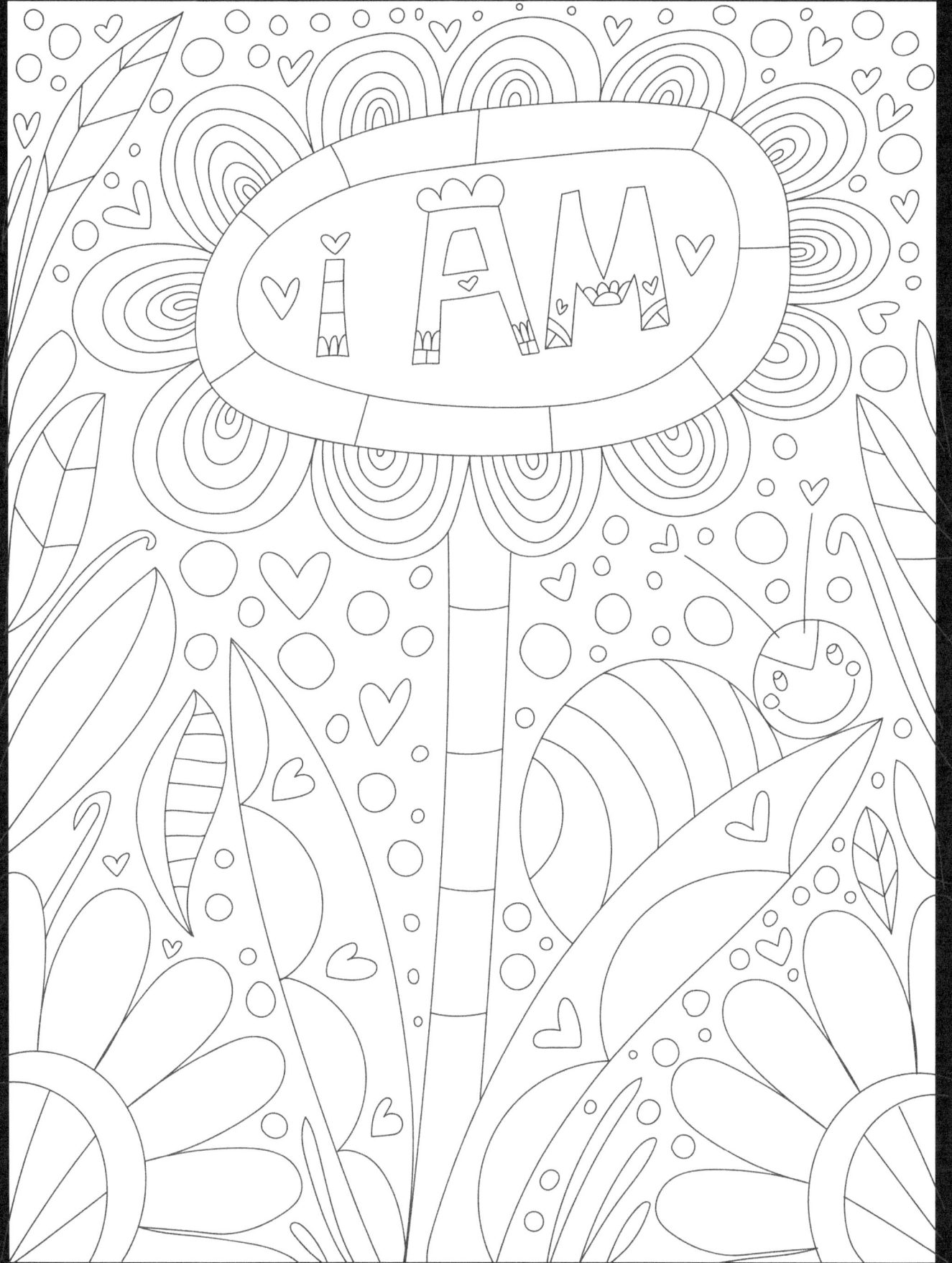

Do things that spark joy in your heart

— Isa Zapata

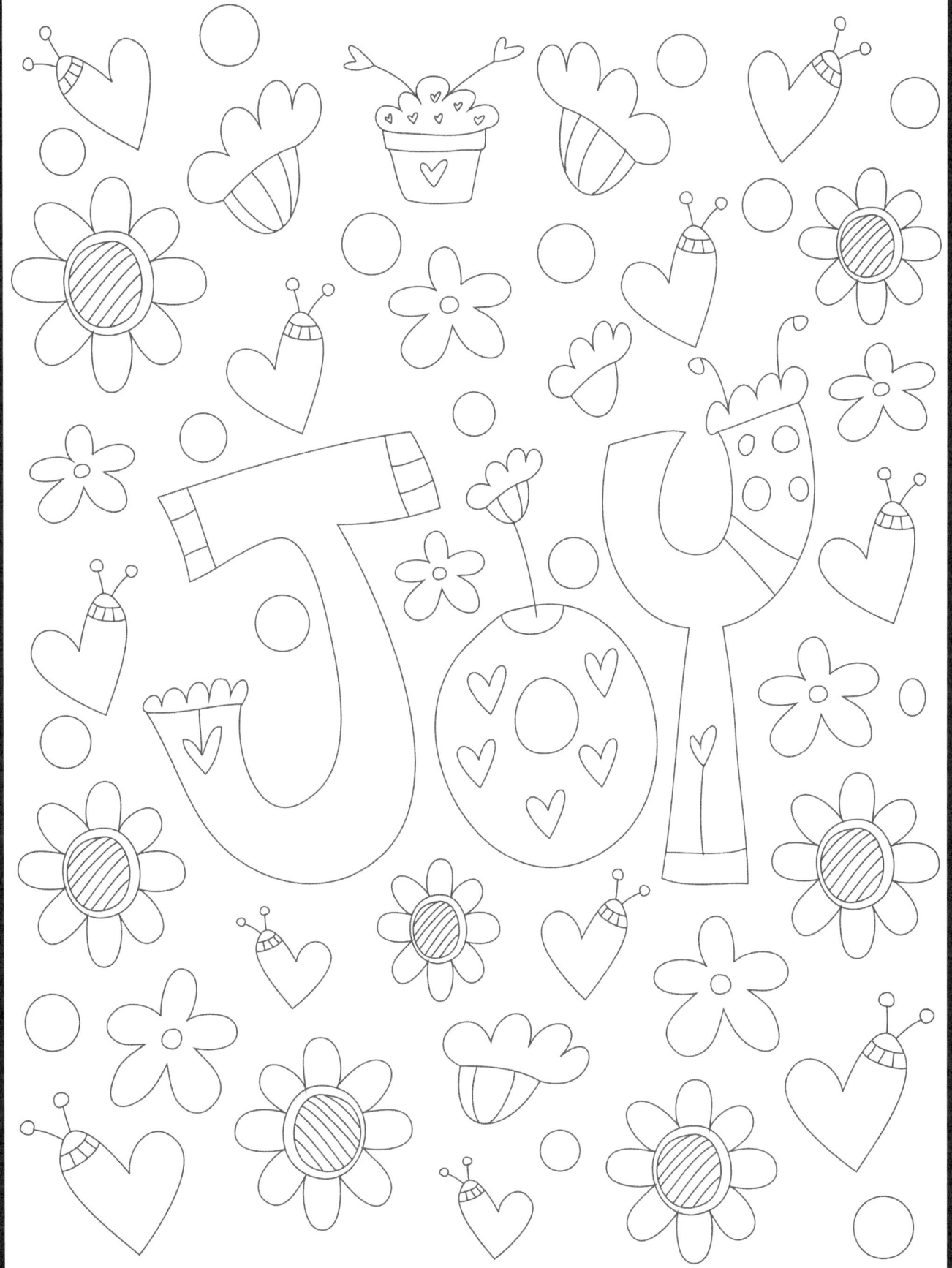

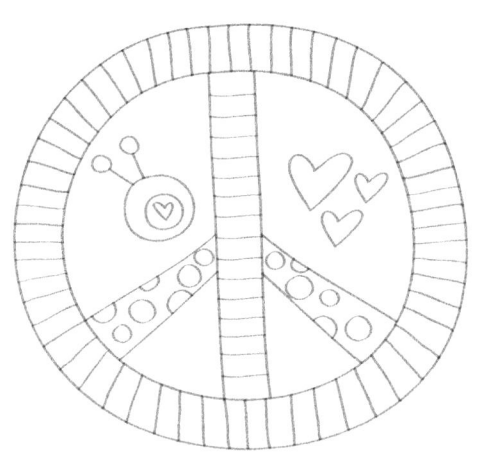

I FIND JOY IN THE LITTLE THINGS

When we better ourselves we are improving our world

— Isa Zapata

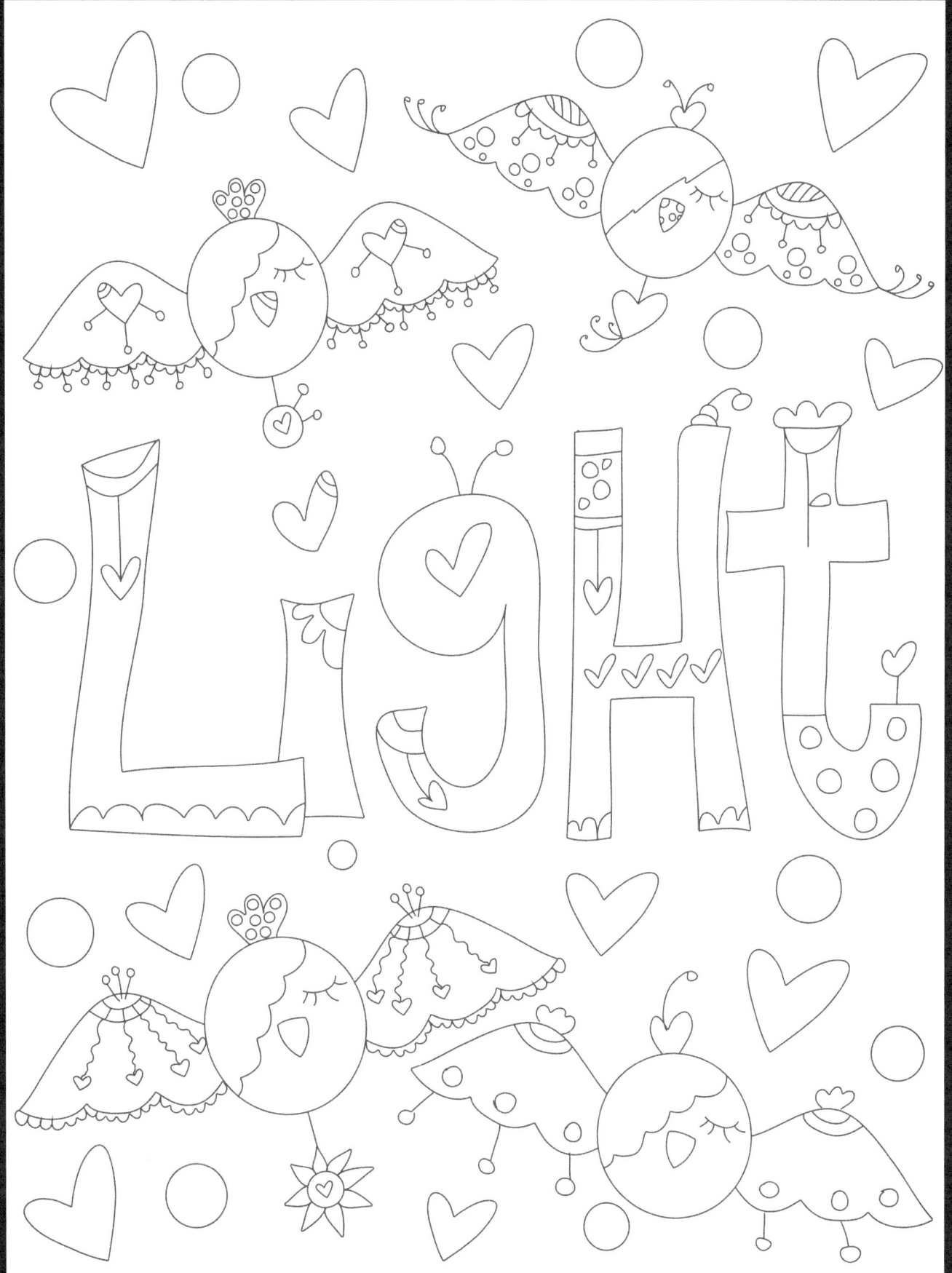

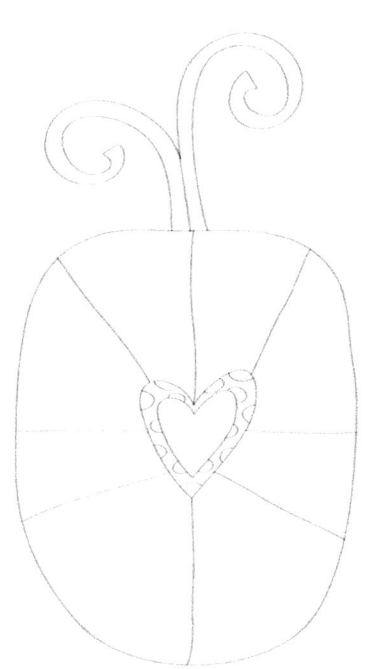

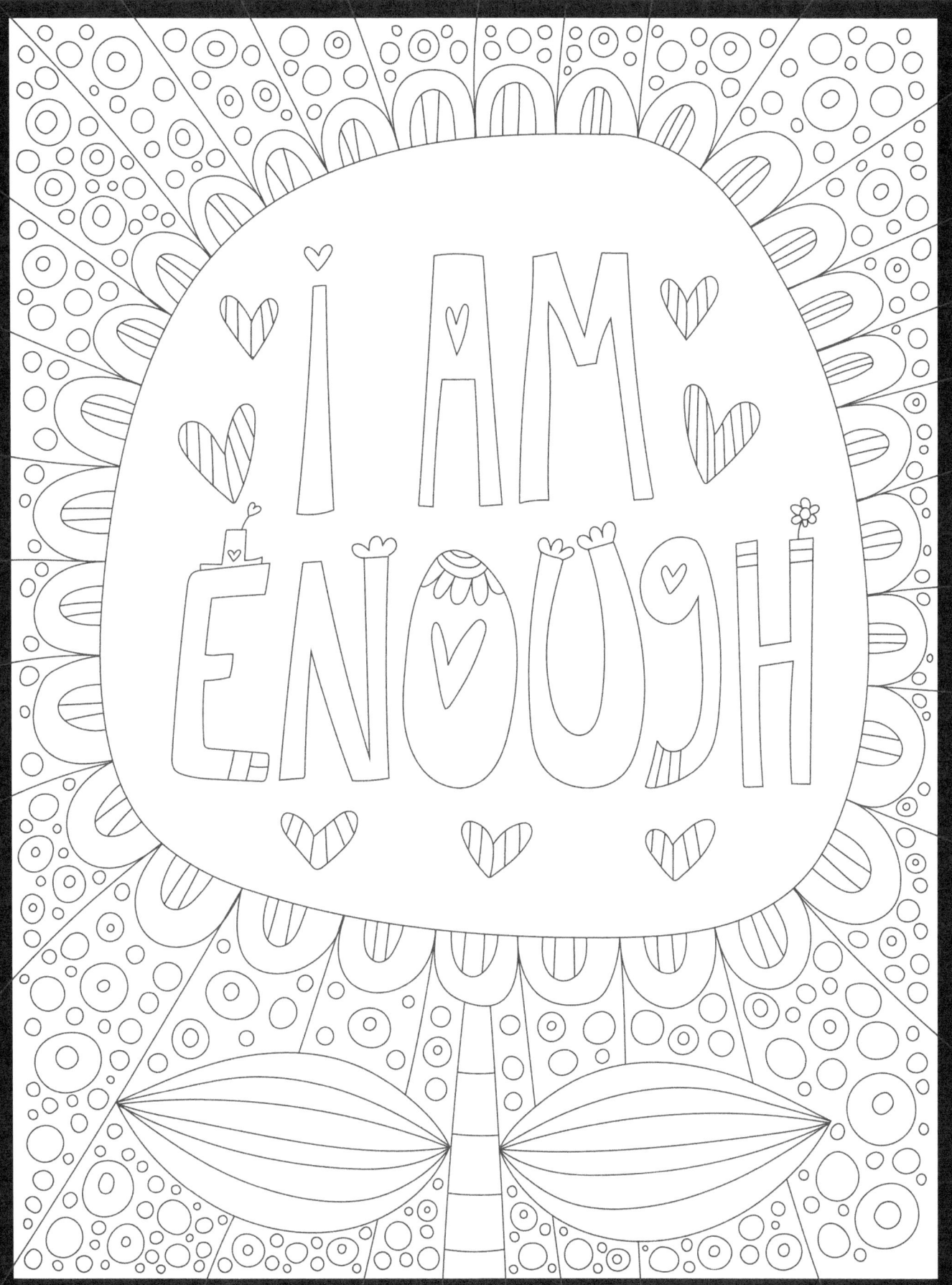

BE LOVE AND YOU'LL BE SURROUNDED BY it

―― ISA ZAPATA ――

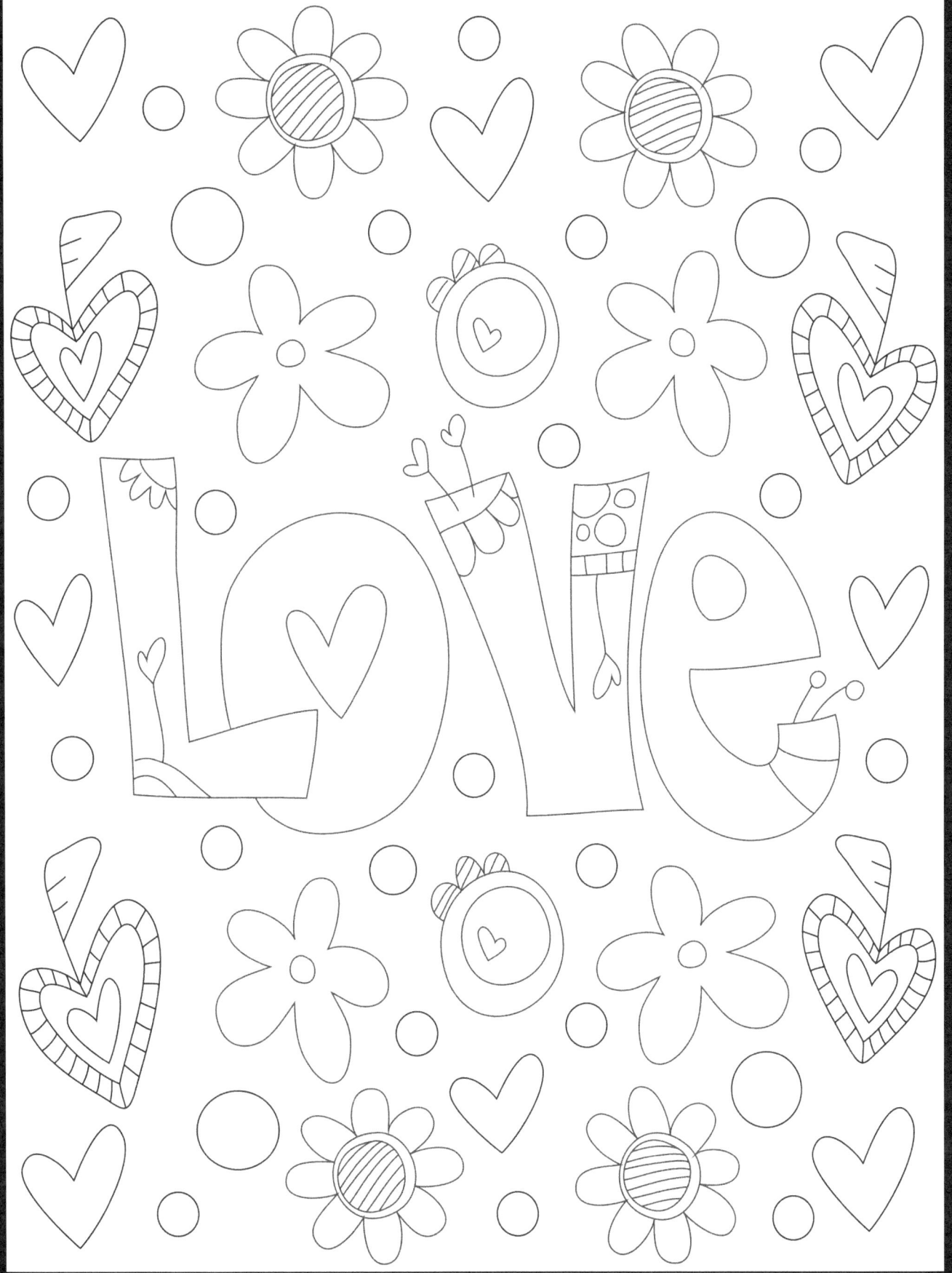

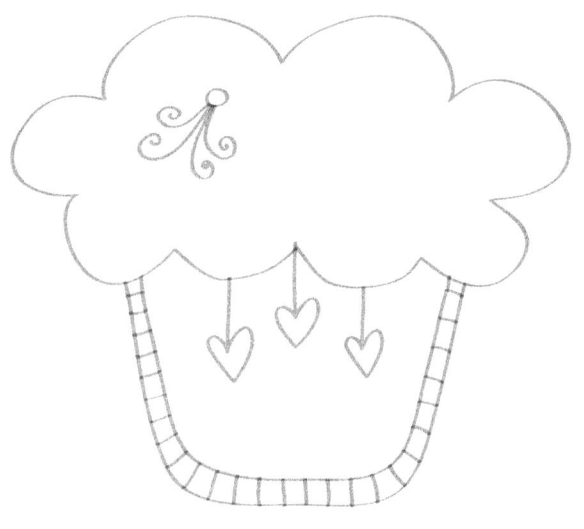

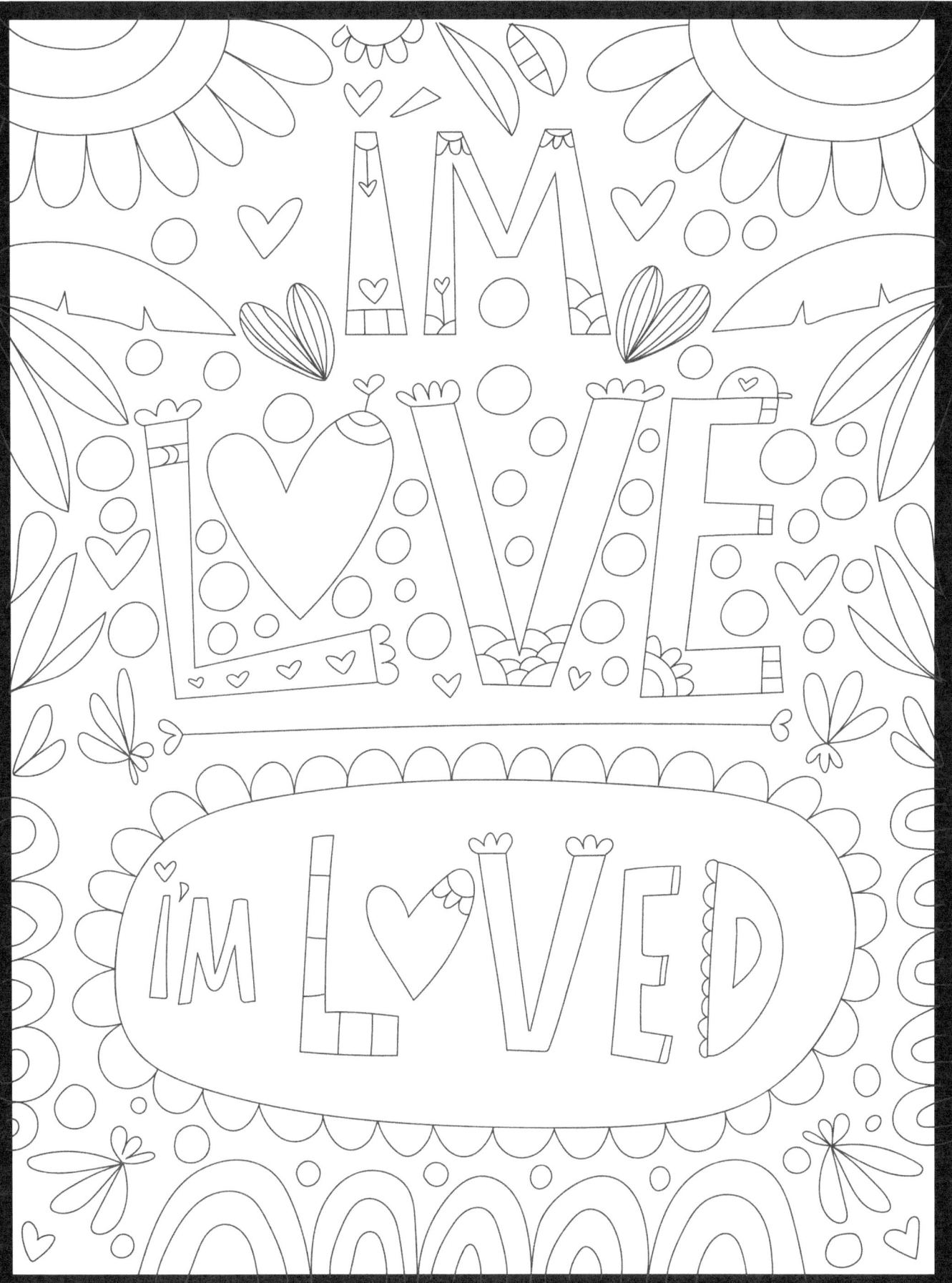

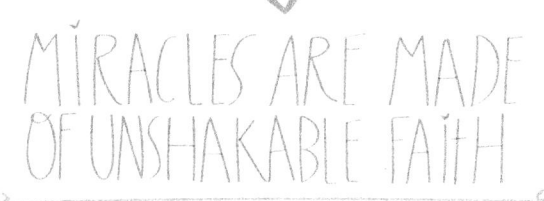

MIRACLES ARE MADE
OF UNSHAKABLE FAITH

- ISA ZAPATA -

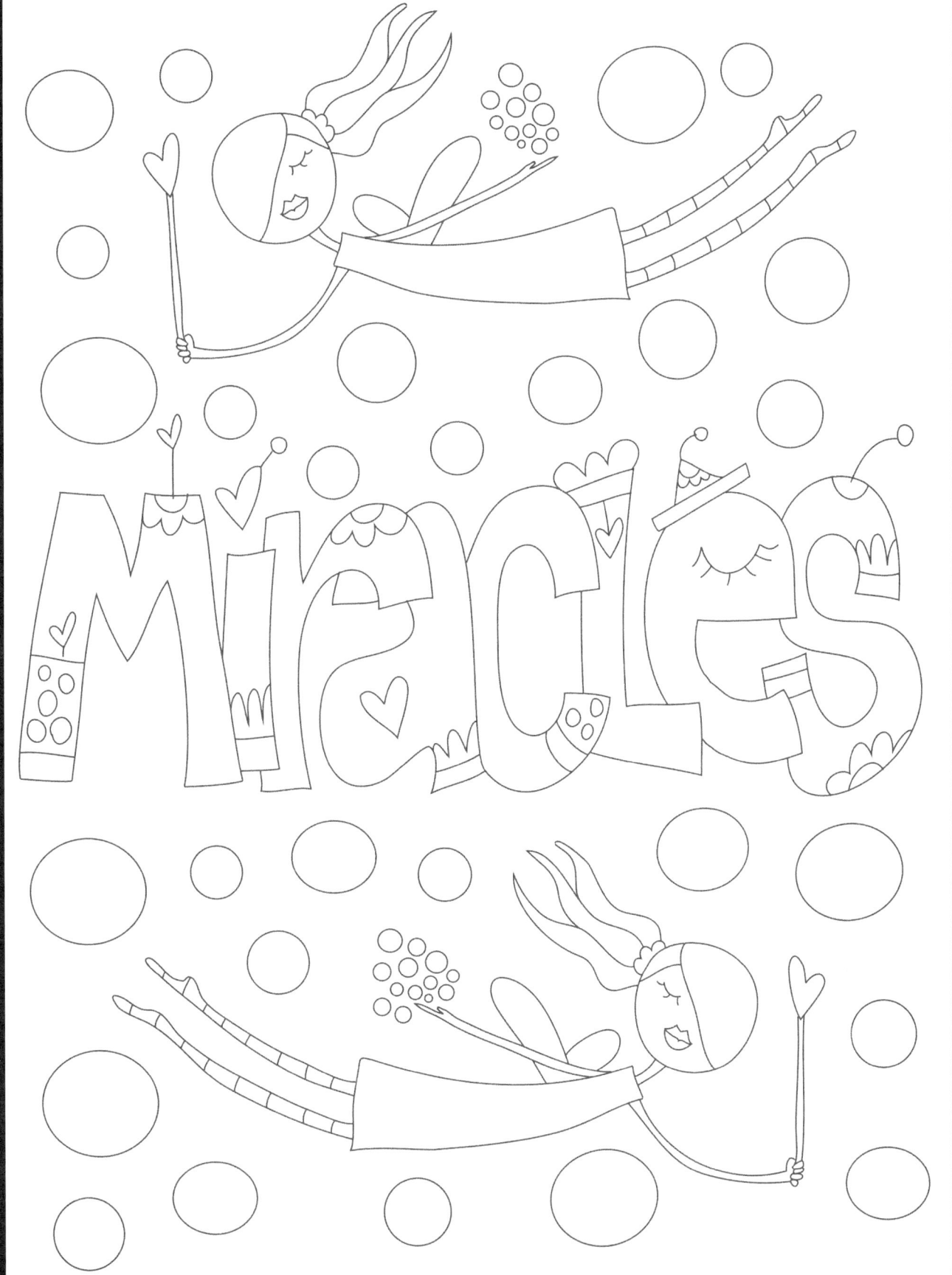

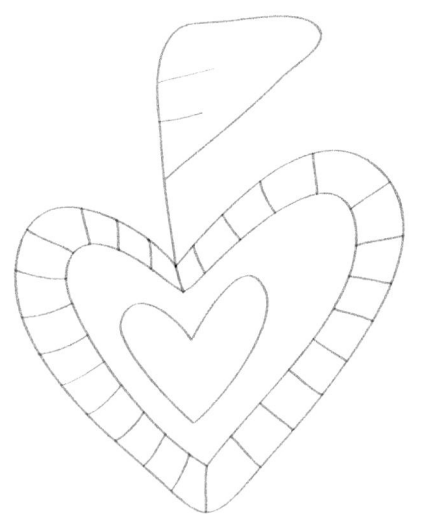

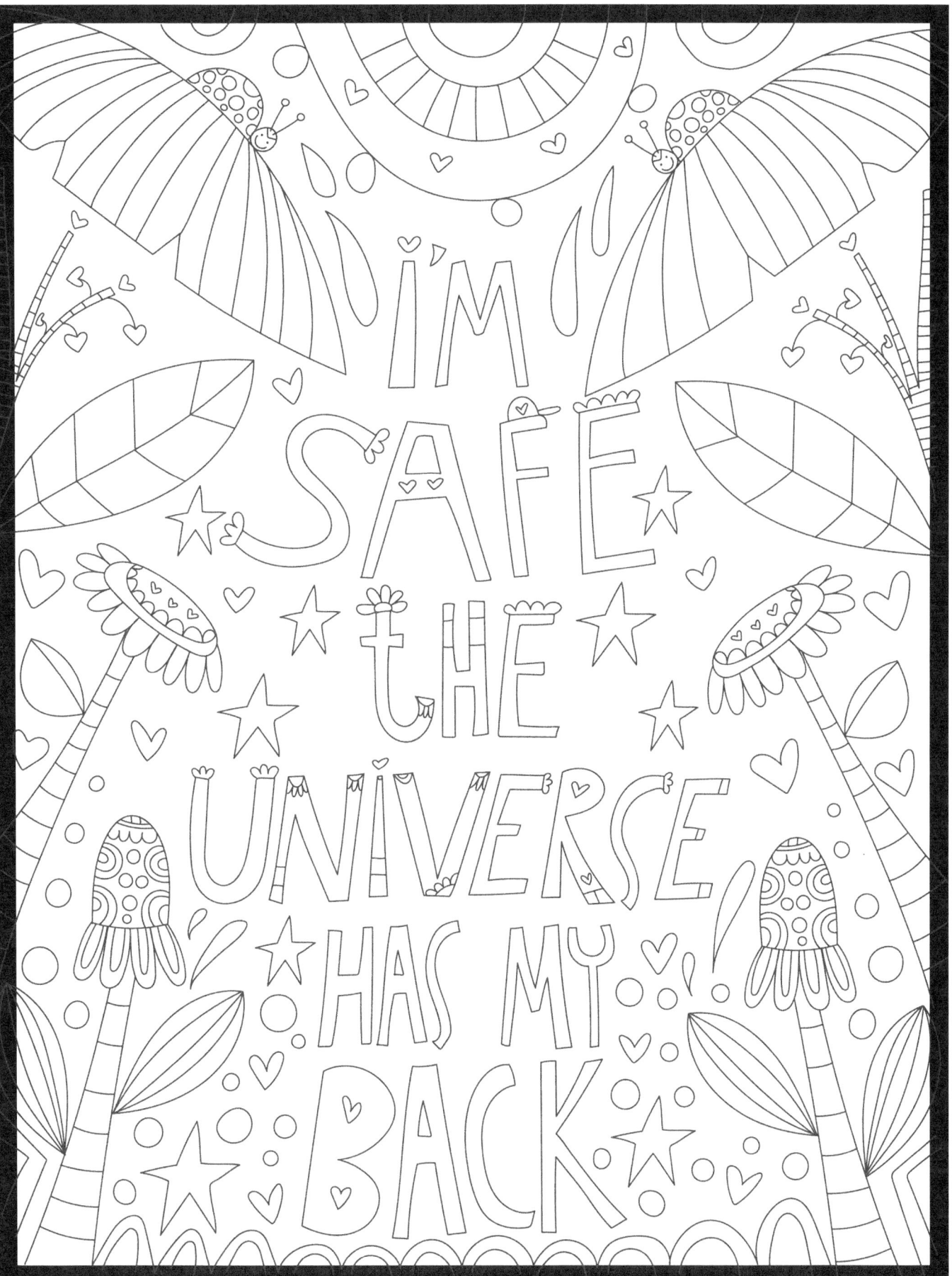

PEACE IN THE WORLD
WILL COME WHEN
WE ARE AT PEACE WITH OURSELVES

— ISA ZAPATA —

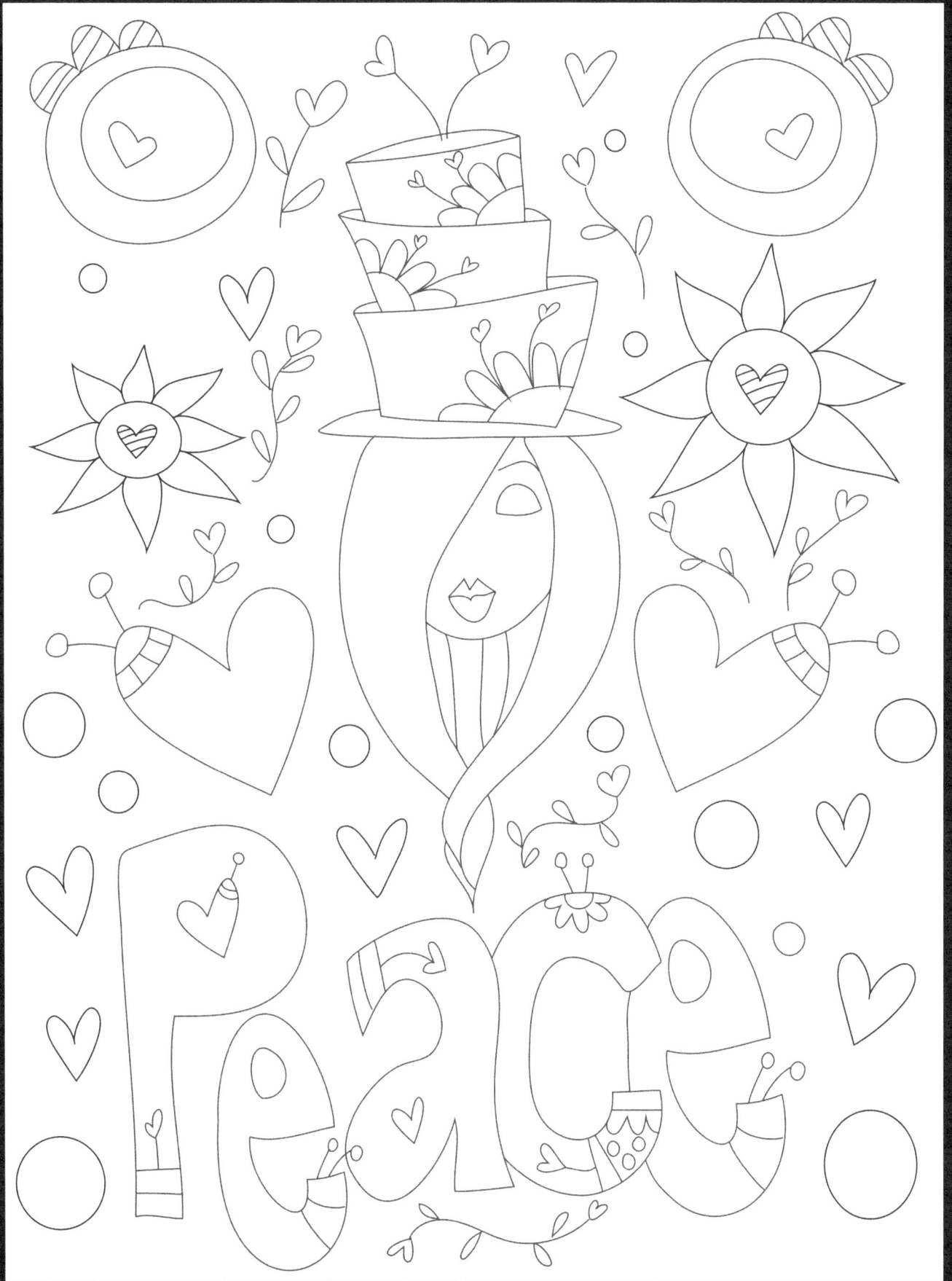

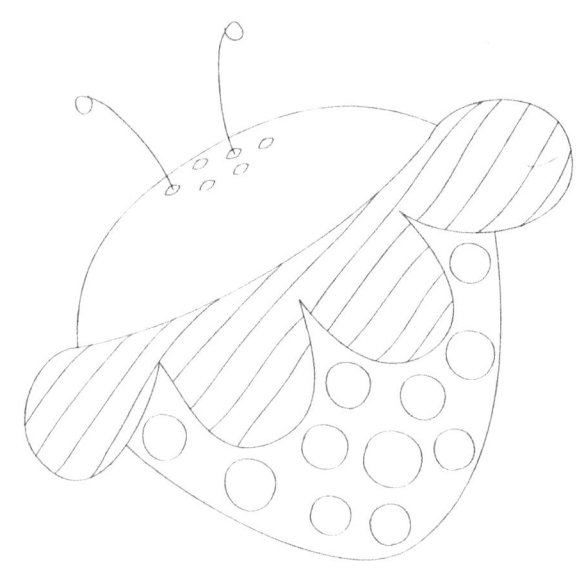

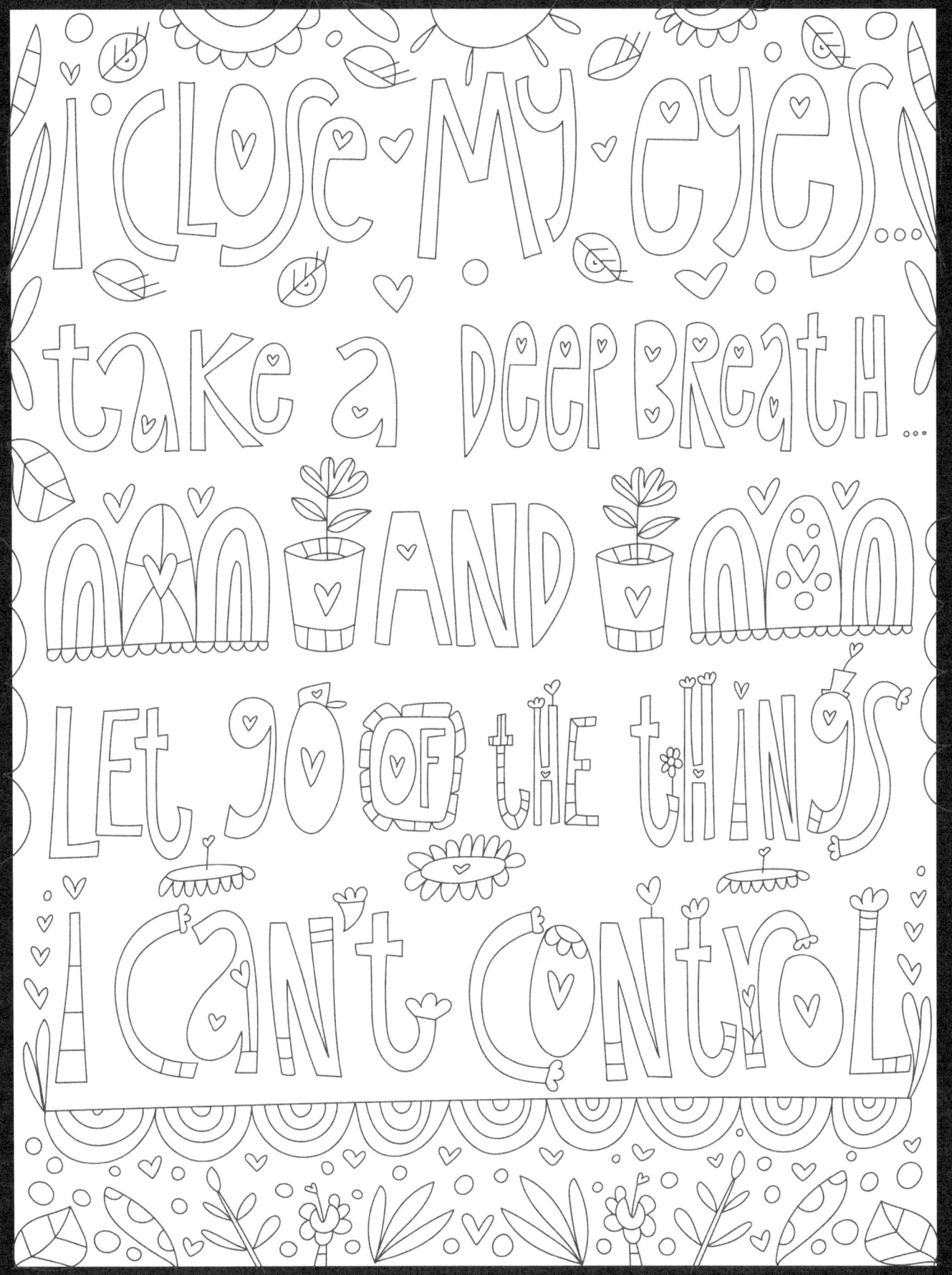

FAITH IS THE SWITCH THAT TURNS THE IMPOSSIBLE INTO POSSIBLE

— ISA ZAPATA —

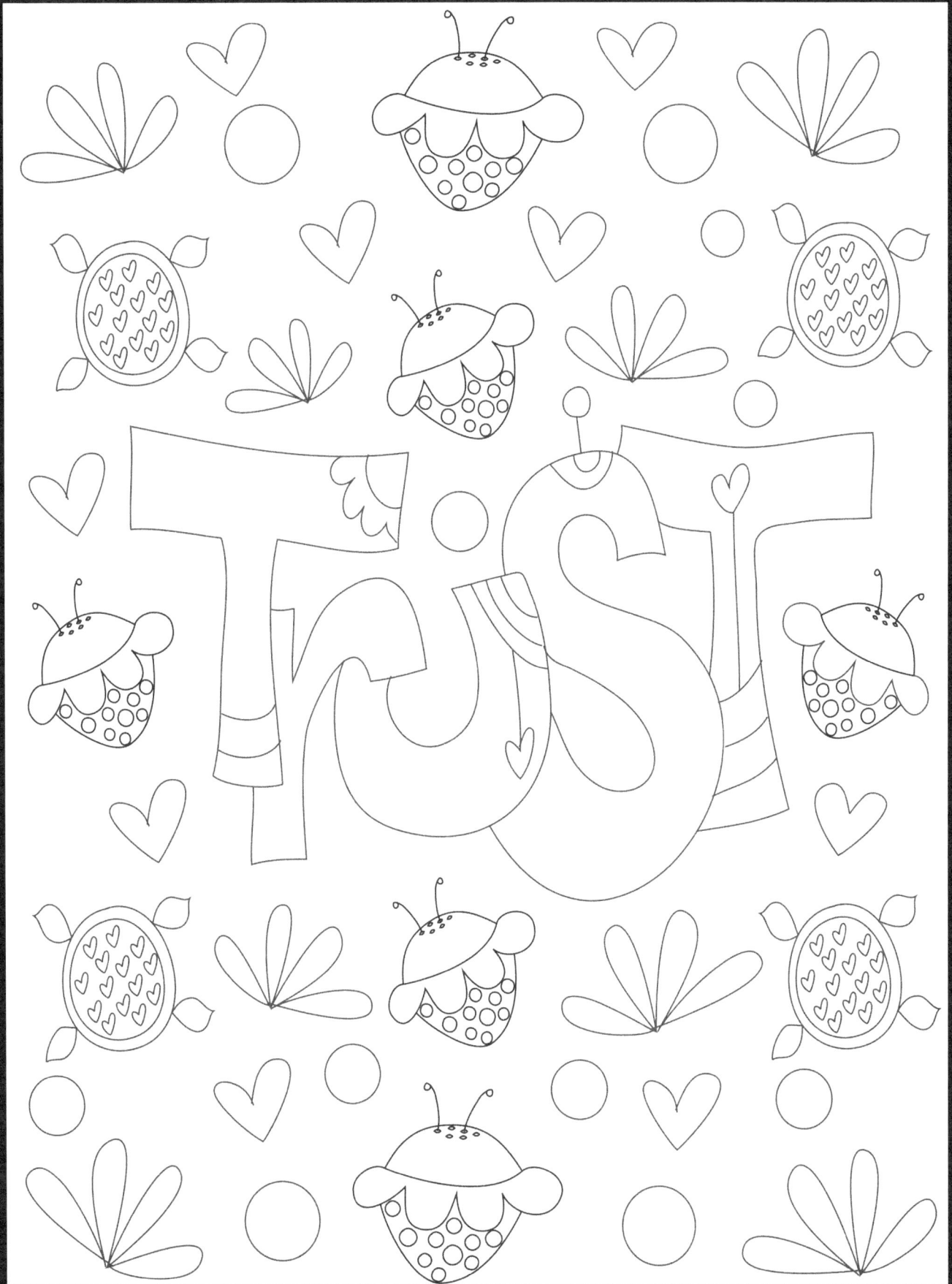

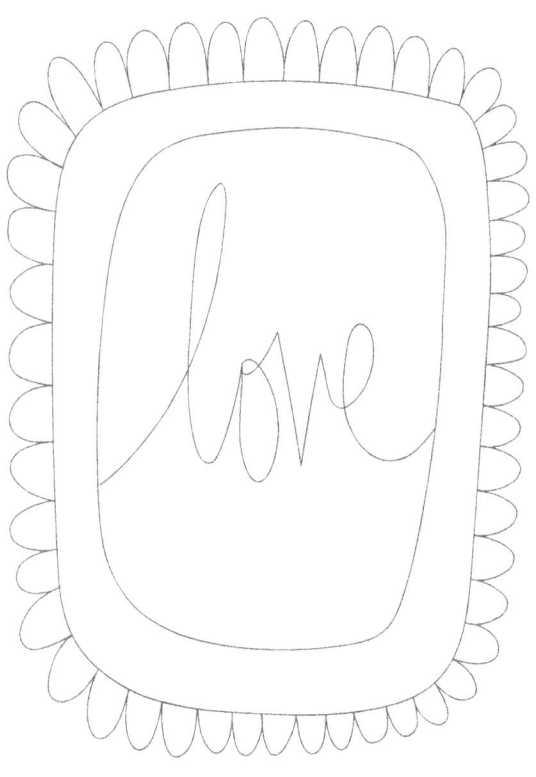

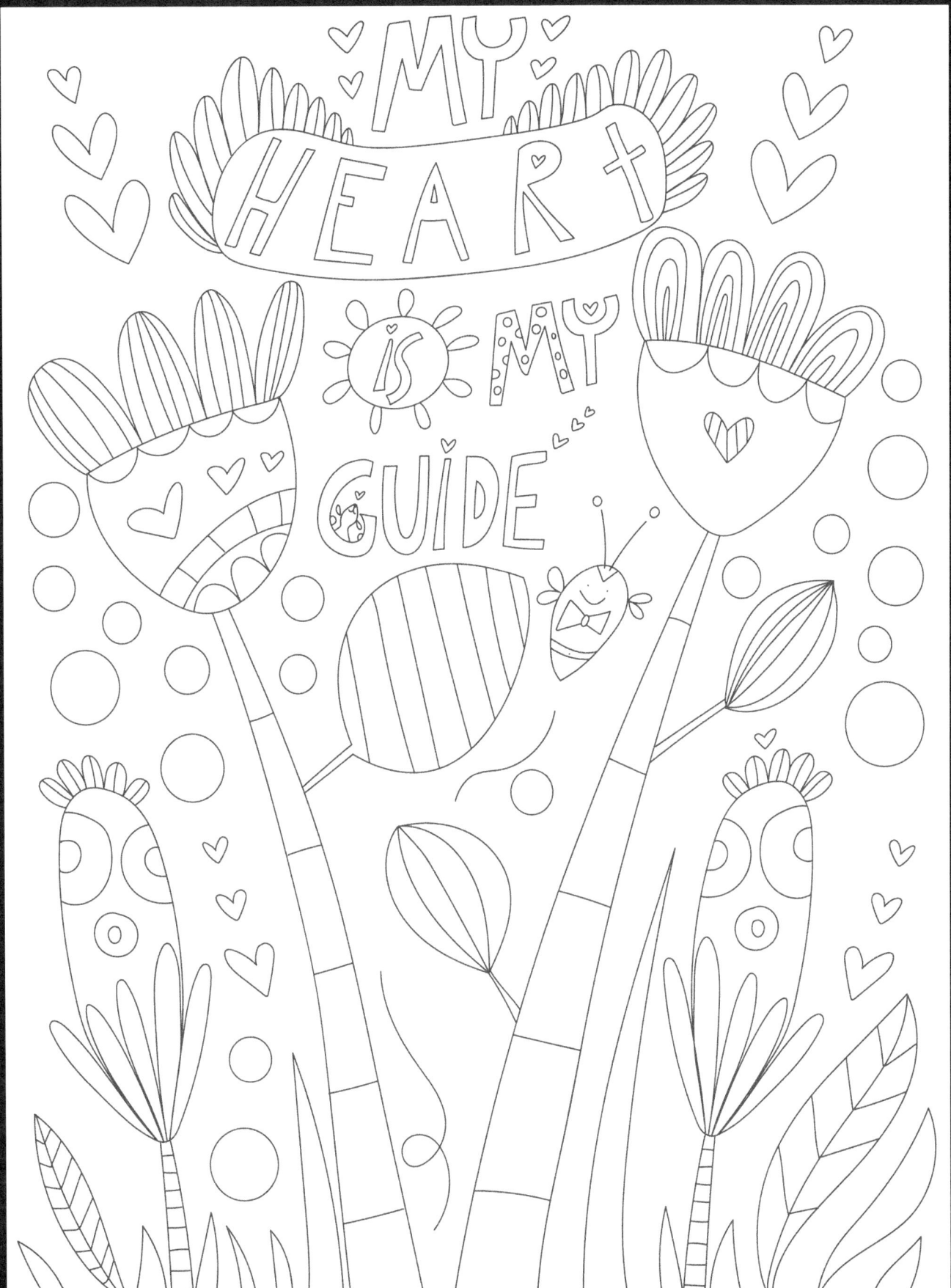

COMPASSION STARTS WITH OURSELVES

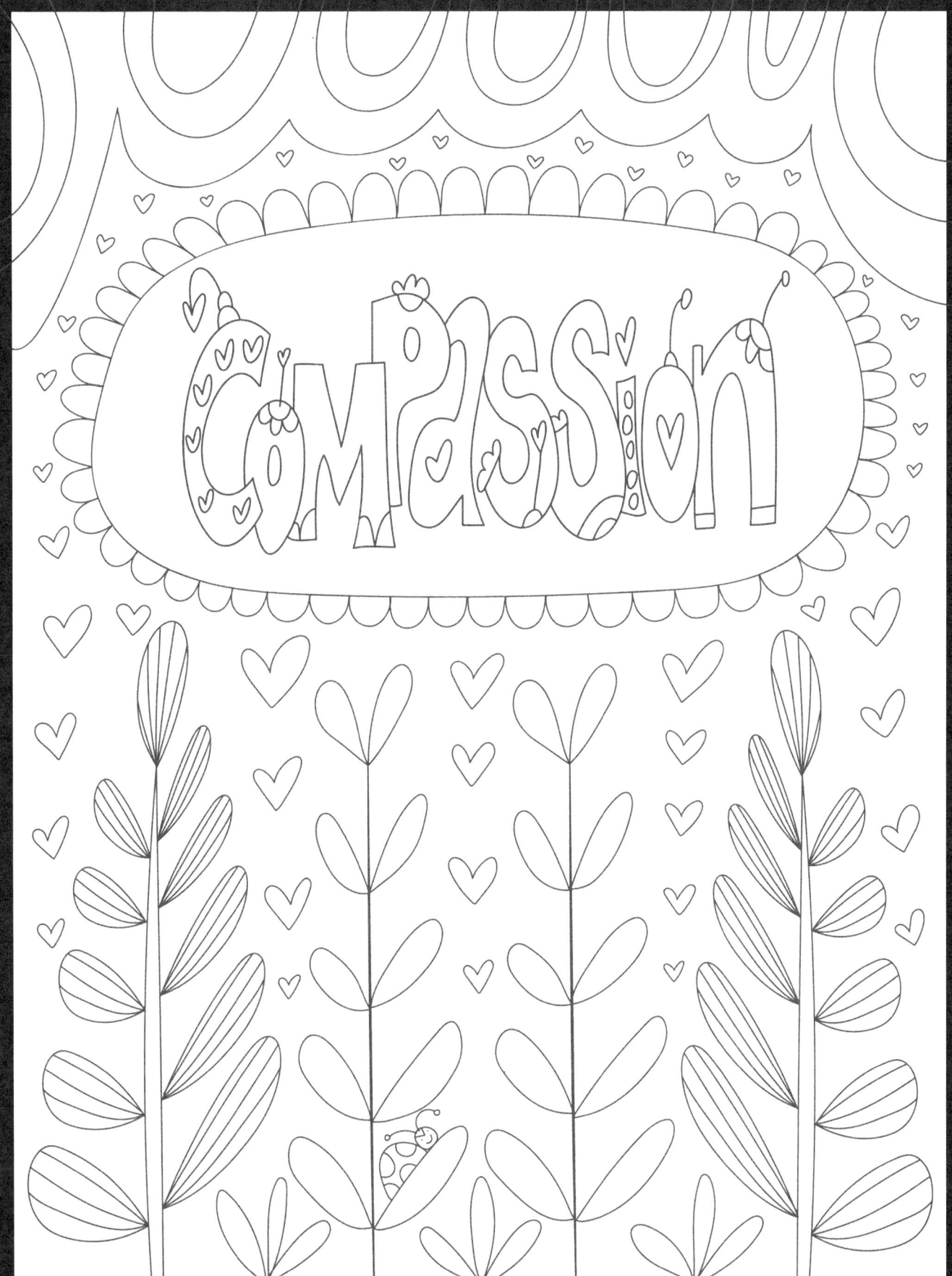

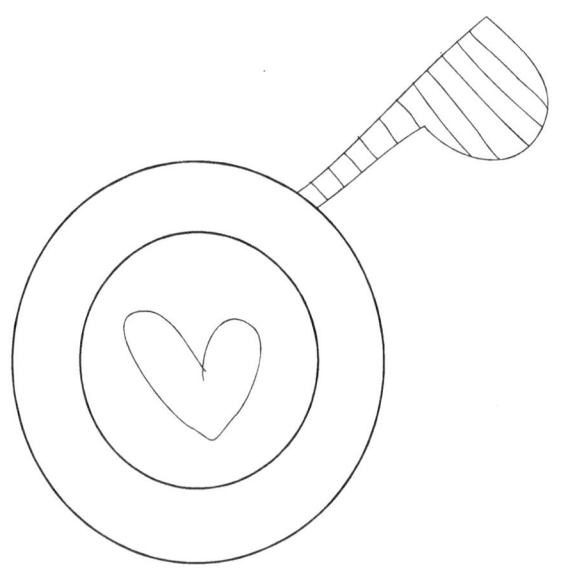

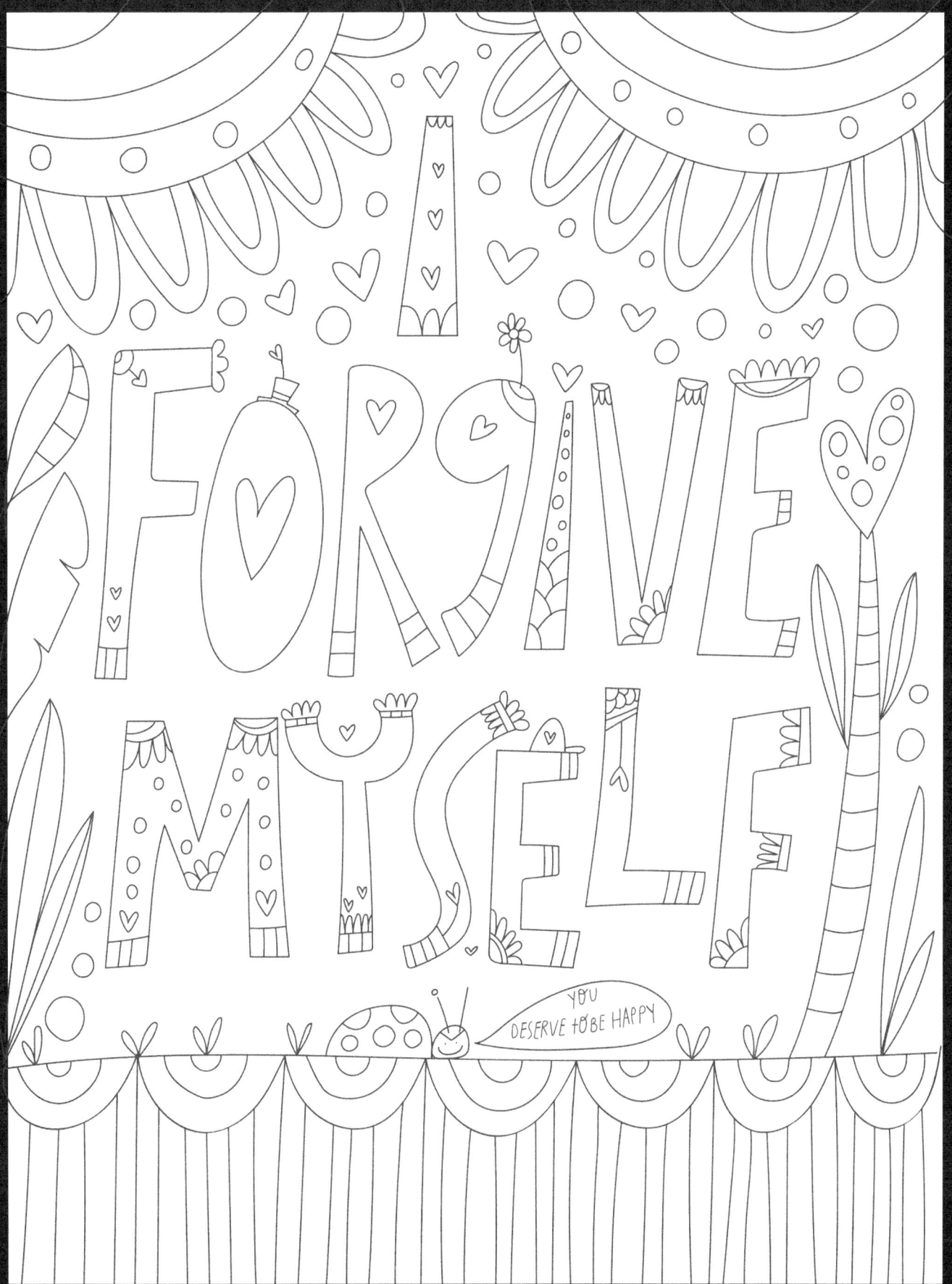

EMBRACE YOUR UNIQUENESS

Acceptance

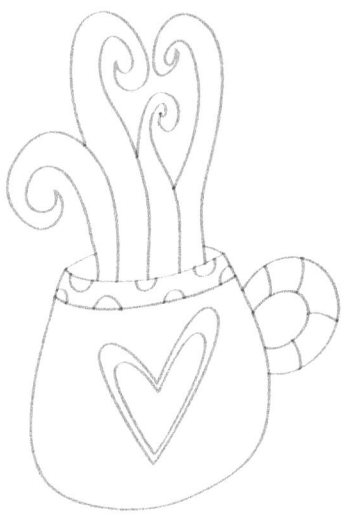

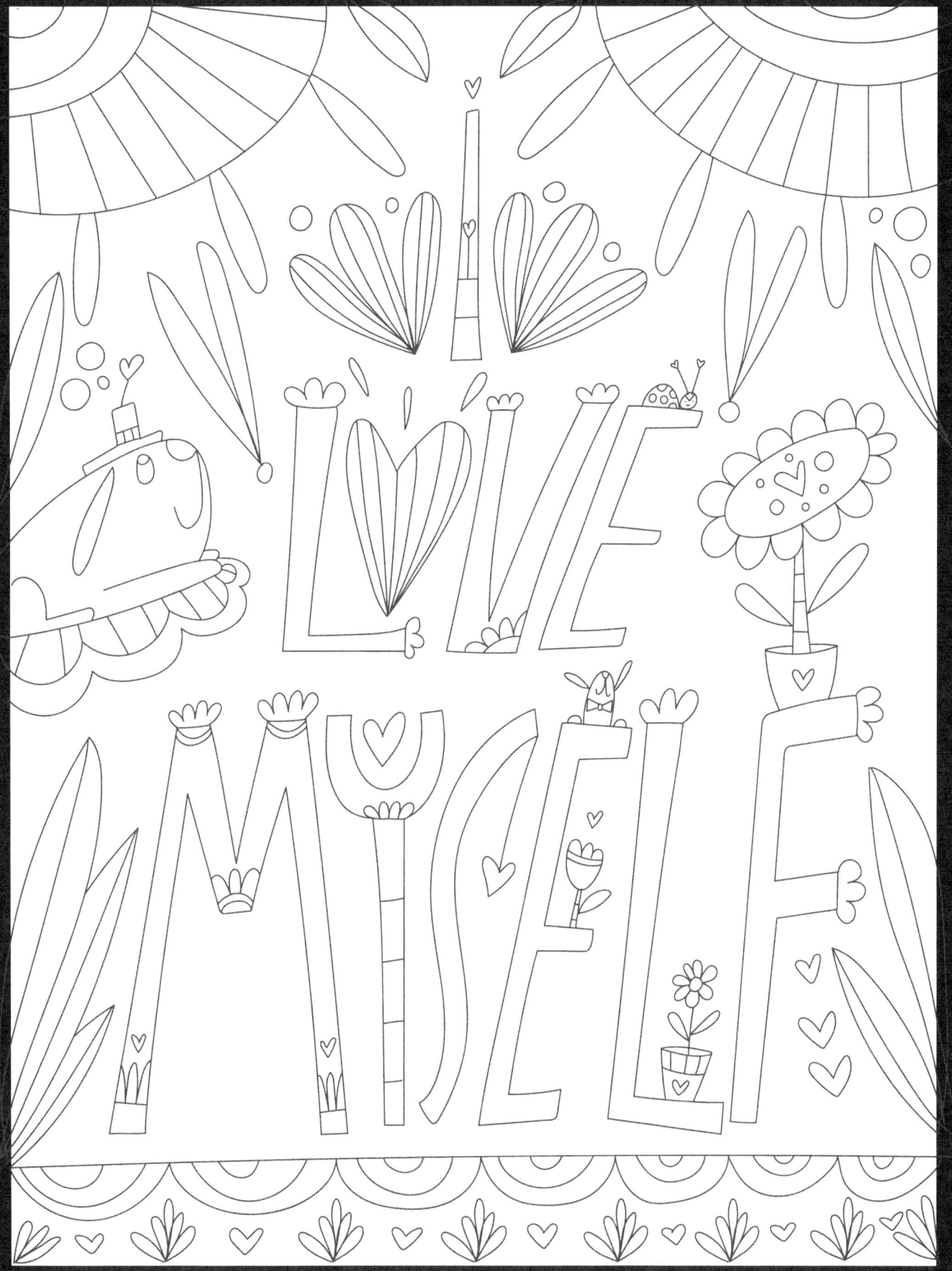

♡

Wisdom comes when we close our eyes, quiet our mind, and let our heart guide us

— Isa Zapata

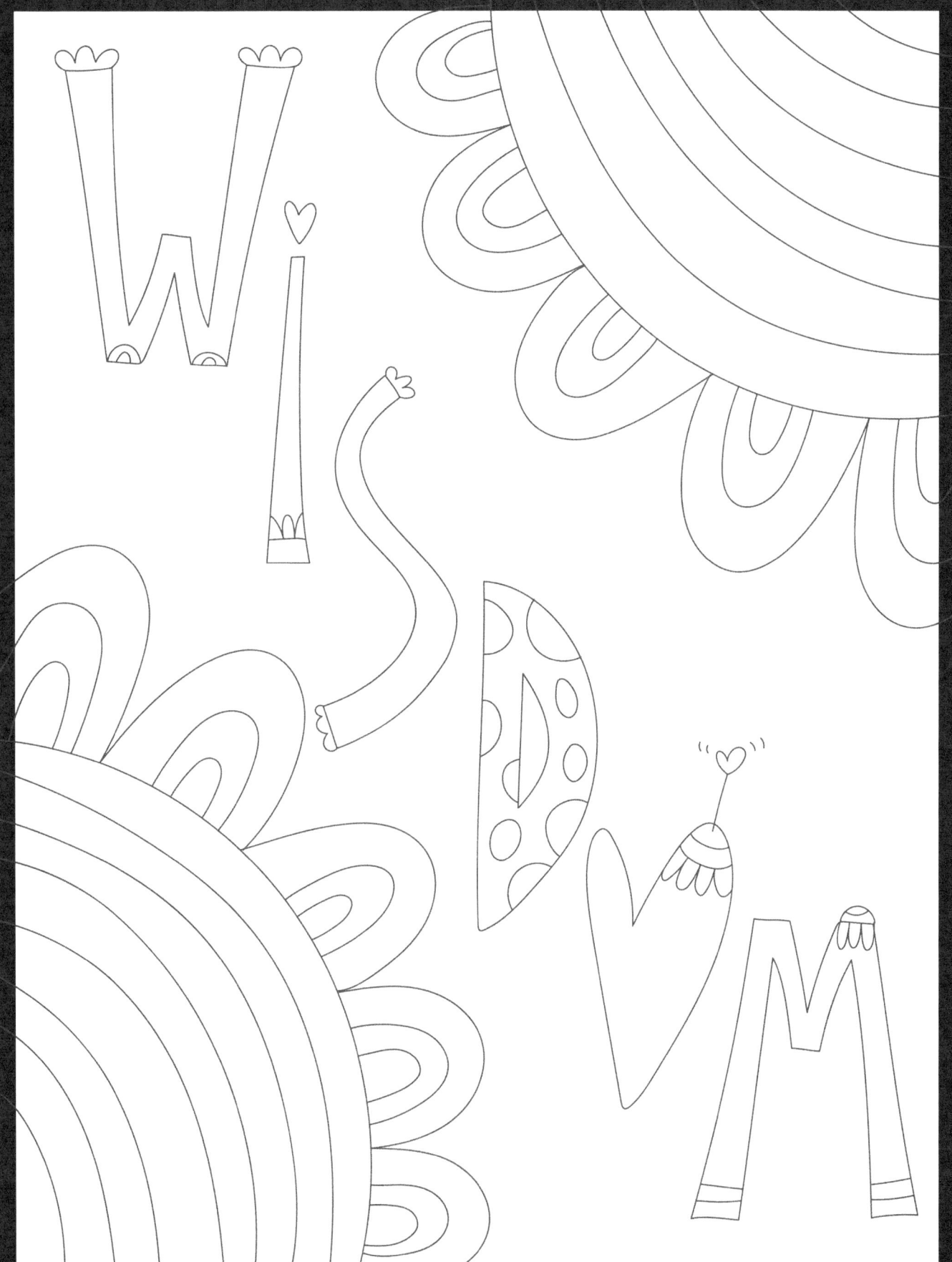

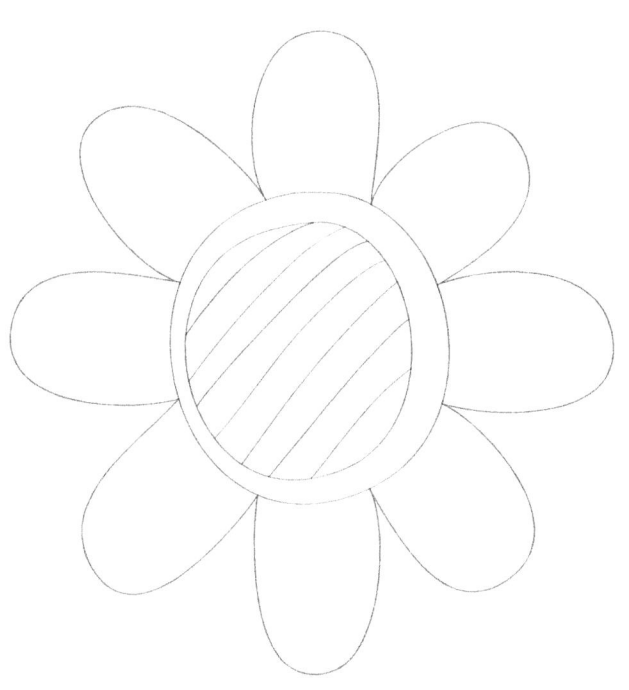

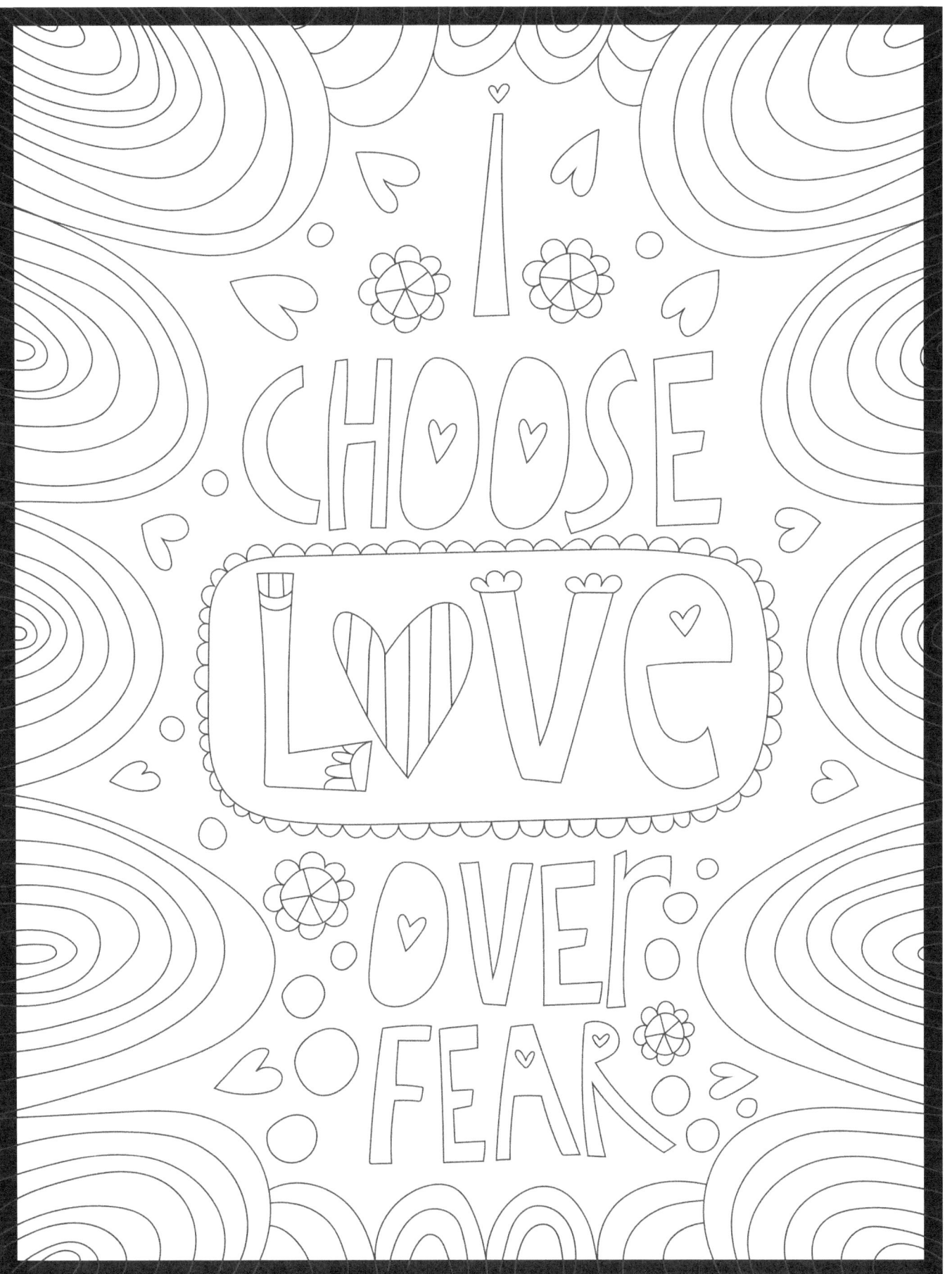

♥

Reset, reinvent and enjoy the process

— Isa Zapata

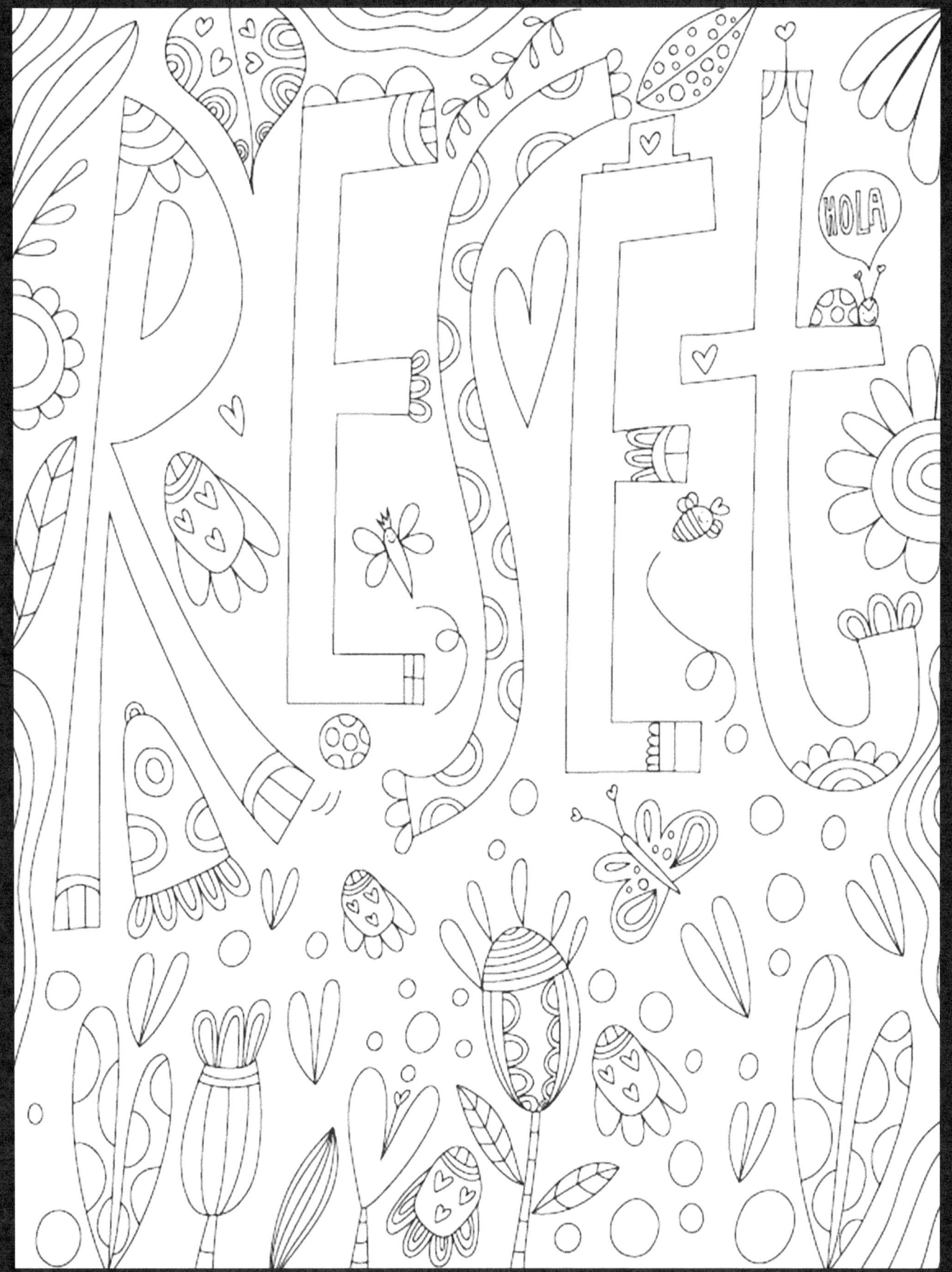

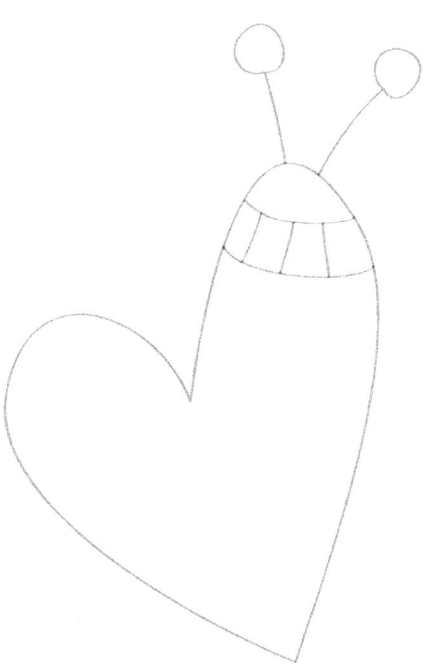

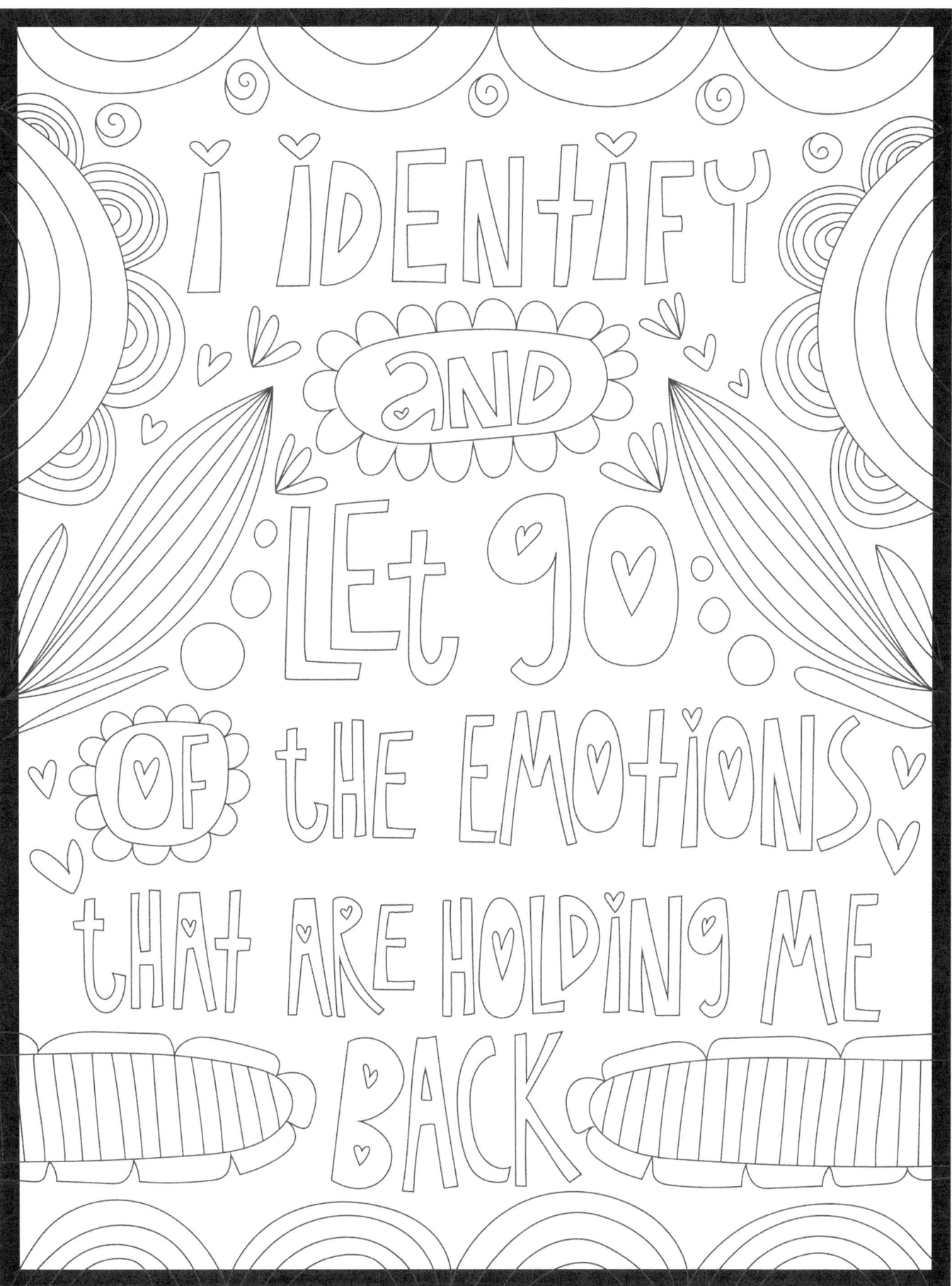

POSITIVE THOUGHTS +
POSITIVE FEELINGS =
POSITIVE OUTCOMES

—ISA ZAPATA

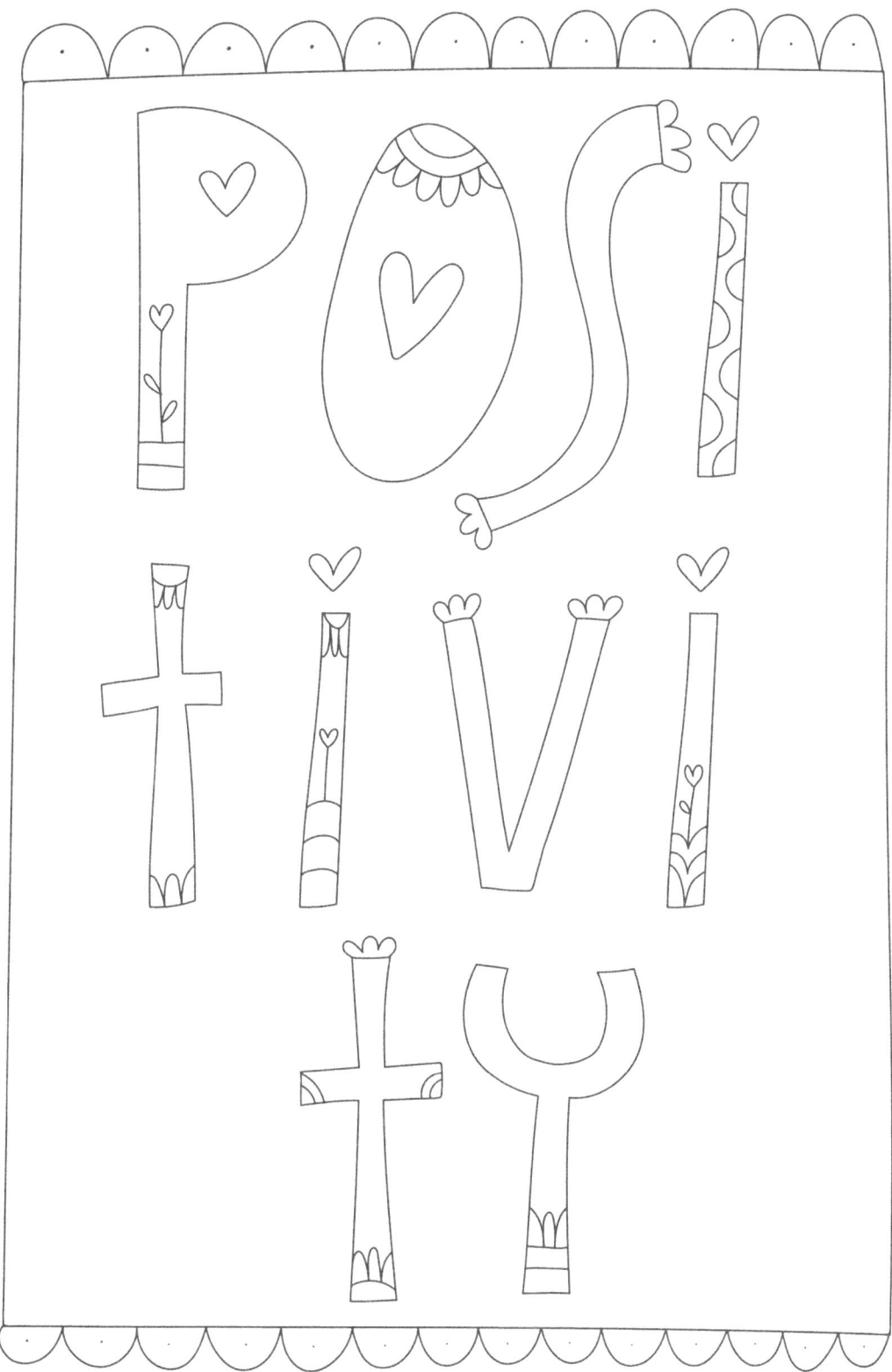

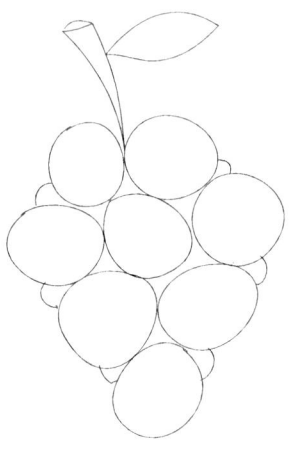

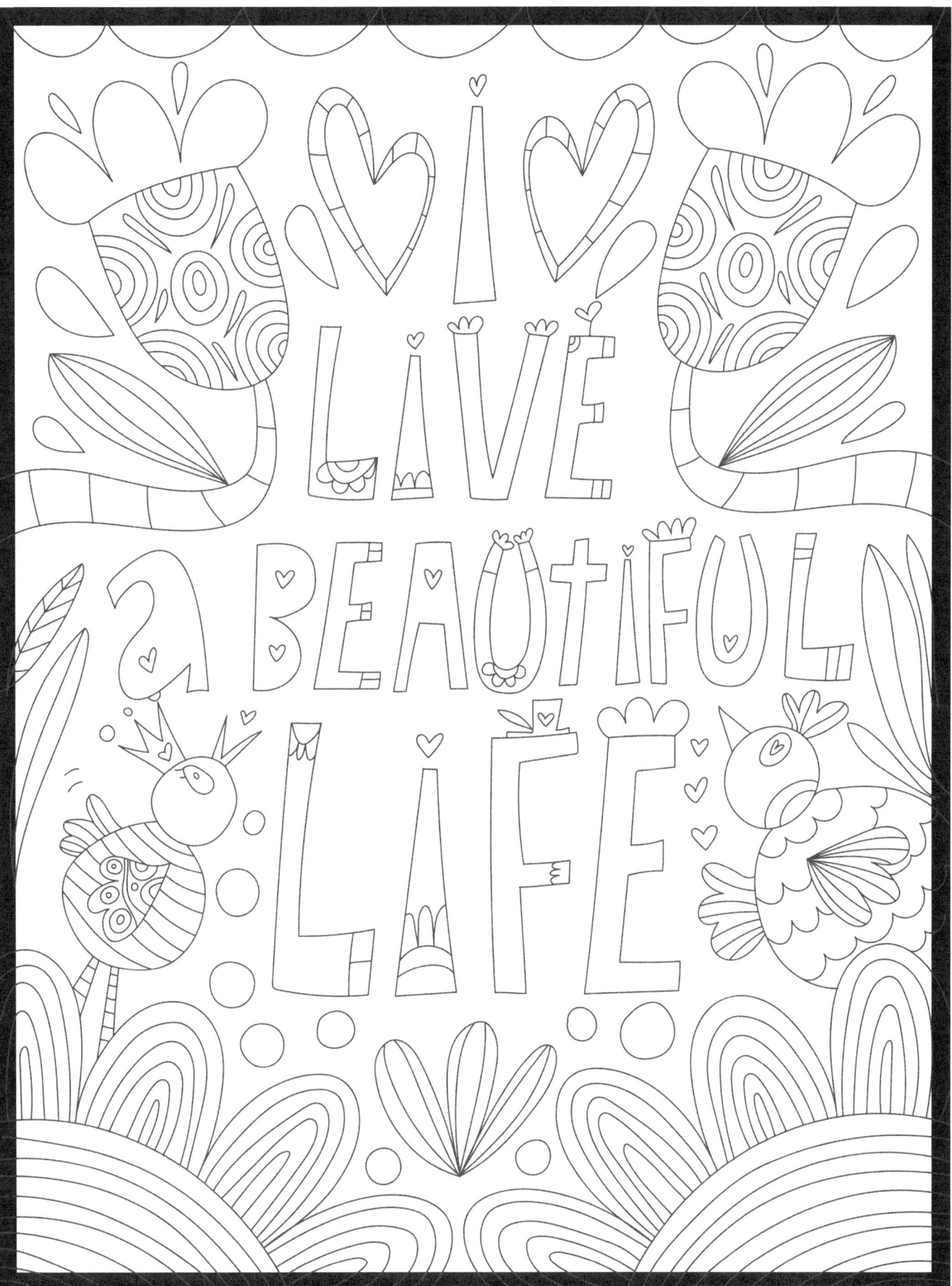

The more I open my heart and know myself, the more blessings I receive

—Isa Zapata

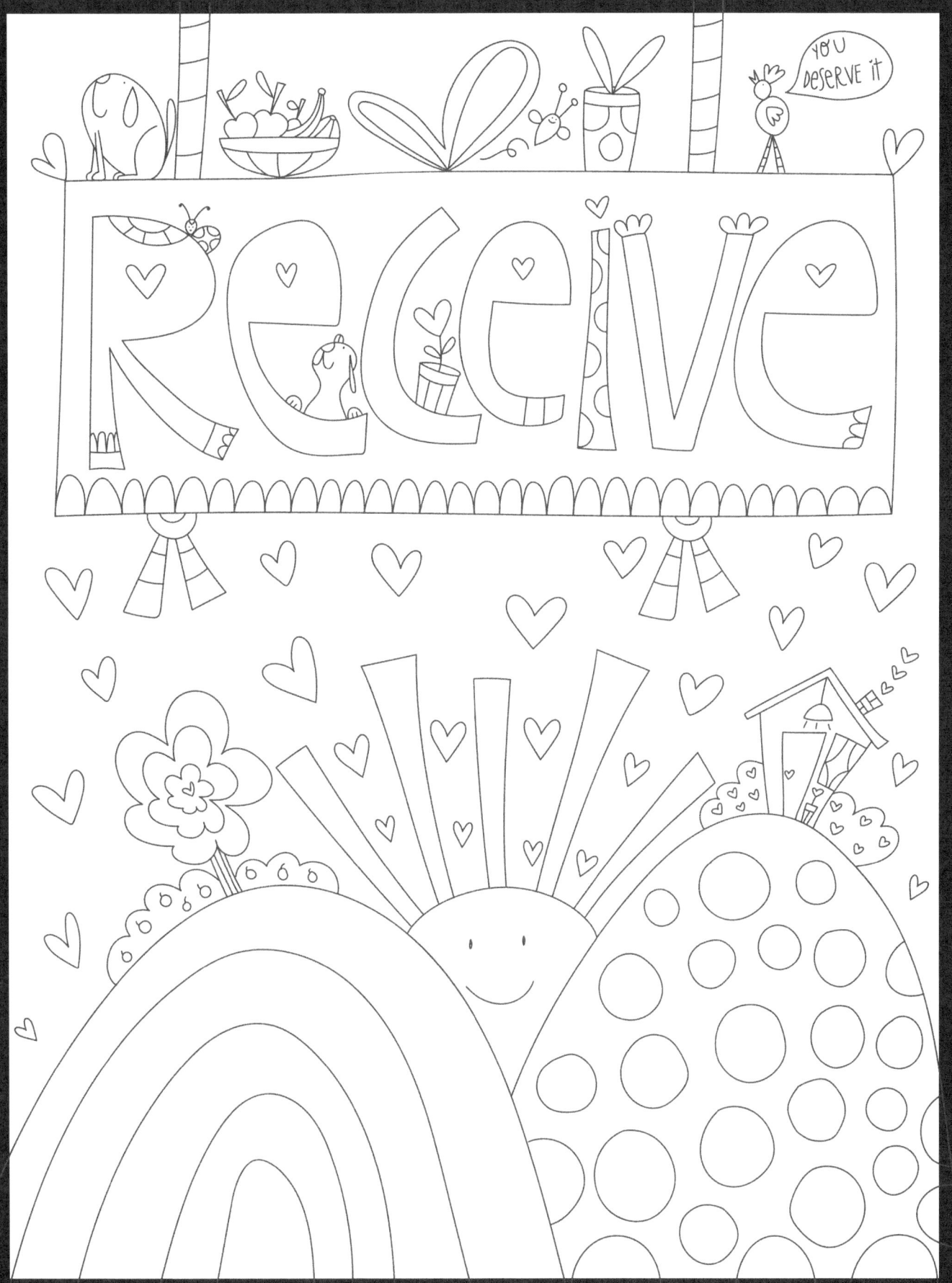

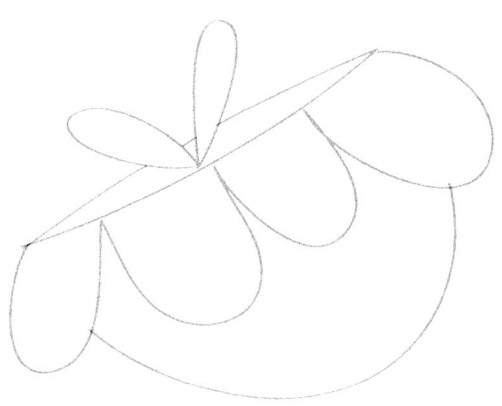

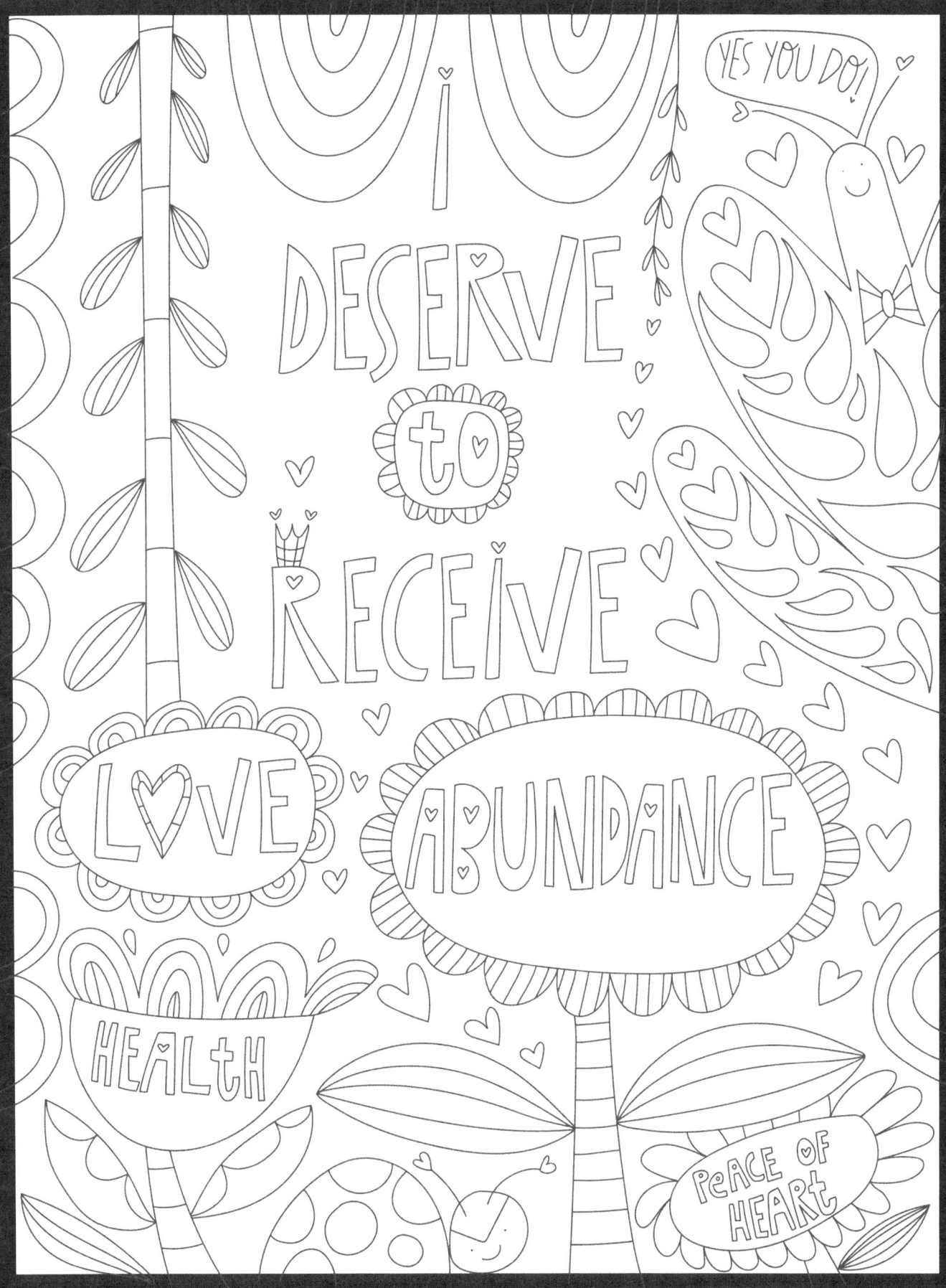

♥
Goals must come from our hearts, not from our ego

— Isa Zapata

I BELIEVE IN MY GOALS

NAME

DATE

- DAILY HABITS
- PERSONAL
- HEALTH
- LIFE PURPOSE
- FINANCES AND CAREER

FILL OUT THE WHITE SPACES WITH YOUR GOALS WITHIN EACH CATEGORY

www.ingramcontent.com/pod-product-compliance
Lightning Source LLC
Chambersburg PA
CBHW060002230526
45472CB00008B/1905